# Everything Your Heirs Need to Know

## Organizing Your Assets
## Family History
## Final Wishes

---

### THIRD EDITION

---

## David S. Magee
## John Ventura

**Dearborn**
Financial Publishing, Inc.®

This publication is designed to provide accurate and authoritative information in regard to the subject matter covered. It is sold with the understanding that the publisher is not engaged in rendering legal, accounting, or other professional service. If legal advice or other expert assistance is required, the services of a competent professional person should be sought.

Editorial Director: Cynthia A. Zigmund
Managing Editor: Jack Kiburz
Interior Design: Lucy Jenkins
Cover Design: Design Alliance, Inc.
Typesetting: the dotted i

Dearborn books are available at special quantity discounts to use as premiums and sales promotions, or for use in corporate training programs. For more information, please call the Special Sales Manager at 800-621-9621, ext. 4384, or write to Dearborn Financial Publishing, Inc., 155 North Wacker Drive, Chicago, IL 60606-1719.

## DEDICATION

To Dorothy
and our heirs
with love
—David Magee

To Jaime, Jose, Jennifer,
and my godchild Julia,
with affection
—John Ventura

# PRAISE FOR PREVIOUS EDITIONS

Winner of the Publishers Marketing Association's 1992 Benjamin Franklin Award

"Ingenious and invaluable"

—*Los Angeles Times*

"Could help unravel the technical aspects of wills, trusts, probate, taxes and estate planning in general."

—*The Washington Post*

"The most complete organizer we've seen. Highly recommended."

—*Personal Finance*

"This could prove to be an invaluable asset in your home."

—*San Francisco Chronicle*

"*Everything Your Heirs Need To Know* is an all-in-one-place book for storing necessary and important information that often isn't discussed, even in the closest of families."

—Gannett News Service

"How to communicate the ownership of a burial plot, the type of funeral, the location of a will, bank accounts, safe deposit boxes, and other assets are matters clearly addressed by David Magee's *Everything Your Heirs Need To Know*... It's likely that such a book could save an estate a lot of money that would otherwise be spent in tracking down assets and attendant papers."

—Stanley W. Angrist, *The Wall Street Journal*

# Contents

**CHAPTER 3    Understanding My Insurance Policies**                                 79

Life Insurance • Medical, Health, Disability, Accident, and
Travel Insurance • Vehicle Insurance • Homeowners and
Other Residence Insurance • Additional Liability Protection

*Forms:*

**CHAPTER 4    Tapping into Other Benefits**                                         93

Social Security • Who Can Qualify for Social Security
Benefits • Applying for Social Security Benefits • Veterans
Benefits • Workers' Compensation • Pensions and Other
Retirement Plans

*Forms:*

**CHAPTER 5    Shedding Light on My Banking and Savings Accounts**                   107

Commercial Banks • Mutual Savings Banks • Savings and
Loan Associations • Credit Unions • ATM and Debit
Cards • Safe-Deposit Boxes

*Forms:*

# Acknowledgments

My entire family has continually encouraged this project and has assisted in the preparation of this book. I gratefully thank my wife, Dorothy, for all of her help and assistance in discussing, planning, and typing the manuscript. My son and my daughters and their husbands have given excellent suggestions, which I have used. My thanks to them—Sandy and Tom Burr, Pat and Rick Yuille, Judy and Richard Dugan, and Dave Magee, Jr. (A special thanks to Judy, who designed, edited, copublished, and nationally publicized the first edition of this book, and who worked extensively on research, updates, and revisions for the second edition.) Herbert A. Milliken, Jr., Howard L. Gay, and John W. Olson were kind enough to take their valuable time to read the manuscript and constructively criticize it. My thanks to Deborah Keating, Raymond J. Kelly, III, Jack Neal, Dr. Jody Cornelius, and Ann Wright for kindly reviewing chapters in their areas of expertise and recommending useful ideas for revising the second edition. Thanks also to Sally Jaeger, Shelly Lowenkopf, Jody Joseph, and many good friends who have offered valuable suggestions and support. Finally, for time spent far and beyond the call of friendship, I thank Richard L. Rapport, MD, for his enthusiastic encouragement and for the many hours he spent editing the manuscript.

—John S. Magee

# *Introduction*

*I*t is hard to imagine that an estimated $10 billion currently sits unclaimed in state treasuries across the country. Yet each year, millions of dollars in stocks, bonds, bank accounts, real estate, insurance proceeds, and other assets are turned over to states by organizations unable to locate the rightful owners.

The bulk of this fortune lies unclaimed because heirs to these assets have no idea their inheritances exist. It is not lack of concern for heirs or for the destiny of personal assets that creates this growing untapped treasure. Certainly most of us would much prefer to see the fruits of our lifelong efforts benefit loved ones rather than land in state coffers.

Why, then, are so many heirs unaware of property intended for them? The answer is simply that many people fail to leave their families a clear record of their assets. The widespread habit of filing important papers in shoe boxes, bottom drawers, and scattered files leaves families searching months, even years, for needed papers and records after someone dies— and the search will not even begin if the family does not know an asset exists.

One California family was recently tracked down by private investigators for a company that had sold stock to their father over 20 years before. Because no record of the $500 in stock was found after the father's death, the family was not aware of his investment. However, thanks to the company's president, who had personally sold the stock to their father and hired the investigators, the heirs were located just one week before the state was to claim the assets. The $500 in stock was worth $160,000! This family was fortunate; *most heirs to unrecorded assets never know their inheritances exist.*

Comedian W.C. Fields was an extreme case. Memories of his impoverished youth brought Fields recurring nightmares about being stranded in a strange city without funds. The wealthy performer recalled opening as many as 700 bank accounts, often in fictitious names, in the cities he visited around the world. Fields left no record for his heirs and only 48 of his bank accounts were located after his death. Over a million dollars of his estate is thought to have remained scattered in hundreds of undiscovered bank accounts.

While few of us have 700 bank accounts (much less the million to put in them), we may have picked up a couple of life insurance policies, bought a few shares of stock, or opened an extra savings account or two over the years. We also can probably locate the papers to prove it, perhaps with a little digging. The question is whether anyone else can.

## WILLS ARE NOT ENOUGH

A will that fully outlines the assets you own will take care of this problem, right? Not necessarily. In the first place, few people think to update their wills with each acquisition or sale of personal property. Also, many wills simply divide estates into bulk portions, mentioning major assets and leaving heirs, executors, and the courts to determine the remaining contents of the deceased's estate. Without clear records, the family is faced with the burdensome and often costly task of locating records, papers, and documents to establish the content and value of the estate.

Furthermore, certain major assets are not even typically included in wills. Life insurance proceeds, pensions, Social Security, and veterans benefits, for example, all have fixed plans of distribution unaffected by wills, and so they are not commonly mentioned in them. Therefore, a clear, up-to-date, comprehensive listing of all your available assets and your benefits can be invaluable to your heirs. This book is designed to make that information easy to provide.

One of the kindest things you can do for your family is to spare them needless frustrations and stressful decisions at the time of your death. Many people live together for 50 years without discussing their wishes regarding life support, organ donations, funeral or memorial services, burial, or cremation. Without intent, they leave many distressing decisions for their loved ones. You can make your death easier on your family simply by deciding on and recording your own preferences. A will, however, is not the best place for detailing such wishes, because your will may not be read until after your burial. This book discusses various arrangements available to you and provides a place to express your wishes.

Perhaps the most cherished legacy you can provide your heirs is your unique knowledge of your family history, your recollections about your own life, interests, and accomplishments, and other special remembrances. You can share these in Chapter 2.

## GUIDING YOU AND YOUR HEIRS THROUGH THIS BOOK

Chapter 1 gives your heirs the emergency information they will need in case of your incapacity or death. The chapter includes a checklist, "A Guide for My Survivors," which leads your heirs through steps that are normally taken in the event of a death and directs them to related information in the book. Two other important lists follow: "Where to Find Records and Keys" and "Persons to Contact."

The first part of each following chapter contains information for you and your heirs. This is followed by forms designed for you to provide your heirs with a detailed personal record of your assets, family history, final wishes, and other notes for your heirs.

You do not need to complete the forms in the order in which they appear. It may be more enjoyable to go through a first time jotting down the information that is readily available. Then you may go back and fill in the missing pieces.

You may find that some forms do not apply to you. If so, indicate that they do not apply and go on. *If the forms do apply to you, fill them in.* Even though you may not have all of the answers at first, take the time to find them. You know the sources; your heirs may not.

Feel free to modify the pages according to your needs. For example, if you are unmarried but have someone significant in your life whom you would like to include, just cross through *spouse* and replace it with the term you prefer to describe your relationship, such as *special friend* or *lifetime partner.*

*Fill in the forms with a soft lead pencil.* If your decisions change as time goes by, it will be easy to erase what you have previously written and insert new directions for your heirs. Or, if you prefer ink, correct with typewriter correction fluid.

*Print legibly.* After all, if you take the time to organize this record for your heirs, you want them to be able to read it.

*Keep the forms up-to-date.* As changes occur, update the forms. It is a good plan to review them at least once a year.

*Store valuable original documents in a safe-deposit box.* File photocopies of these documents as well as other needed papers in your home filing system so they will be readily available to your heirs. If you have stored information on computer, list the file locations and file names in this book, and keep backup disks in a safe place. You may also want to keep hard copies of your computer documents in your filing system as well.

*Discuss this book with your heirs.* They must be aware of its existence, know where it is located, and know what it says in order for it to be of value to them. Although for many people death is a difficult subject to discuss, this feeling should be overcome. Sit down and have a frank and open talk with those closest to you.

It is unlikely that you will be able to complete this guide in one or two sittings. Some information will take extra thought or research. But don't look upon it as a task. If you approach it in manageable sections and view it as a fascinating family project, you will find it can give you great satisfaction to track down bits and pieces of your family history, locate the missing birth certificate, and gradually put your affairs in order. These records can be of great interest and value to you during your lifetime. The greatest satisfaction will be in knowing that if anything happens to you, you will be providing an invaluable guide for your heirs with your notes, your wishes, and the information in this book.

# *Lighting the Way— A Gift to My Heirs*

To my heirs—

I have assembled this book for you, my heirs. In describing my final wishes (Chapter 10), I hope to spare you difficult decisions you might otherwise need to make on my behalf. By detailing my assets and benefits (Chapters 3–8), I hope to ease the process of handling my estate and make you aware of all benefits to which you may be entitled. And by providing my personal and family history (Chapter 2), I wish to share with those who will follow me my memories and my knowledge of those who came before.

In this chapter, you will find "A Guide for Survivors," a checklist for you to follow in the event of my death. You will also find the lists "Persons to Contact" and "Where to Find Records and Keys." Finally, at the end of this chapter, you will find "Notes to My Heirs."

I hope that this book brings you comfort and peace of mind. If so, create your own *Everything Your Heirs Need To Know* to light the way for those you love.

# A Guide for My Survivors

**What to do at time of death:**                                    *Turn to the Following Forms*

☐ Immediately authorize donation of body parts (authorize organ donations *prior* to death).*    161

☐ Contact medical school for body bequeathal.*    162

☐ Contact funeral director or memorial society.    165

☐ Notify friends, relatives, and employer.    9

☐ Maintain a list of flowers, cards, donations, and other expressions of sympathy.

☐ Arrange for friends and relatives to help as needed with childcare, shopping, cooking, telephones, etc.

☐ Arrange funeral or memorial service.    165–66

☐ Arrange for cemetery lot, mausoleum, or crypt.*    163

☐ Provide obituary information to newspaper.    16–17, 48, 50, 70–78

☐ Arrange for after-service luncheon or gathering for friends and relatives.

☐ Obtain a minimum of eight certified copies of death certificates.

**What to do after the funeral or memorial service:**

☐ Send notes to acknowledge expressions of sympathy.

☐ Notify life insurance companies and file claim forms.    84–86

☐ Notify other insurance providers and file claims where applicable.
  • Medical, health, disability, accident, and travel    88–89
  • Vehicle    90–91
  • Residence    87

☐ Apply for appropriate benefits.
  • Social Security benefits    100
  • Veteran's burial benefits and other applicable benefits    101–2
  • Pension benefits    104–5
  • Workers' compensation benefits    103

☐ Meet with lawyer to commence probate proceedings, if needed.    7
  • Take original will and copies of forms in this book.    148–51
  • Assist with inventory of assets, etc.    84–91, 100–5, 111–23, 120–23, 128–30, 133–38

☐ Notify accountant/tax preparer (unless estate lawyer is preparing final tax returns).    7
  • Take copies of appropriate forms in this book.
  • Take copies of recent tax returns.

☐ Notify stockbroker(s).    120
  • Change ownership of joint stocks by removing name of decedent.    120–23
  • Suspend any open orders of the decedent.

☐ Notify banker(s).    111–12
  • Change ownership of joint accounts by removing name of decedent.    111–13

☐ Notify credit card companies. Close accounts and destroy cards. (In some cases, an authorized signer may apply to take over account in his or her name.)    137

☐ Contact airlines to apply for transfer of frequent flyer miles to primary beneficiary (unless otherwise assigned in will).    133

* *If applicable.*

# Where to Find Records and Keys

*Keep original documents that are valuable or irreplaceable in a safe-deposit box. List safe-deposit box and key locations on pages 111–112. Keep copies of originals in your home filing system.*

**Safe-Deposit Box**                 **Other Locations**

### Personal History

☐ Adoption papers _____

☐ Annulment decrees
or judgments _____

☐ Athletic awards _____

☐ Birth certificates _____

☐ Change of name certificates _____

☐ Civic awards _____

☐ Death certificates _____

☐ Divorce decrees or judgments _____

☐ Dramatic awards _____

☐ Educational certificates _____

☐ Educational transcripts _____

☐ Marriage certificates _____

☐ Military awards _____

☐ Military separation papers _____

☐ Naturalization papers _____

☐ Newspaper articles _____

☐ Organization awards _____

☐ Organization membership
certificates _____

☐ Other _____ _____

☐ _____ _____

☐ _____ _____

### Insurance

☐ Life insurance policies _____

☐ Medical and health insurance
policies _____

☐ Residence insurance policies _____

# Where to Find Records and Keys *(continued)*

**Safe-Deposit
    Box**

**Other Locations**

### Insurance (continued)

☐  Vehicle insurance policies _____

☐  Other _____ _____

☐  _____ _____

### Other Benefits

☐  401(k) agreements _____

☐  IRA agreements _____

☐  Keogh plan agreements _____

☐  Medicare card _____

☐  Military separation papers    (See *Personal History.*)

☐  Pension agreements _____

☐  Railroad retirement documents _____

☐  Social Security card _____

☐  Workers' compensation award _____

☐  Other _____ _____

☐  _____ _____

☐  _____ _____

### Banking and Savings

☐  Cash _____

☐  Checking account statements _____

☐  Credit union account
     statements _____

☐  Savings account books
     or statements _____

☐  Other _____ _____

### Securities, Real Estate, and Miscellaneous Assets

☐  Business records _____

☐  Decrees _____

☐  Deeds _____

☐  Home improvement records _____

# Where to Find Records and Keys *(continued)*

| Safe-Deposit Box | | Other Locations |
|---|---|---|

**Securities, Real Estate, and Miscellaneous Assets (continued)**

☐ Judgments _____

☐ Leases _____

☐ Mortgages _____

☐ Patents or copyrights _____

☐ Rental property records _____

☐ Stock brokerage statements _____

☐ Vehicle certificates of title _____

☐ Other _____ _____

**Will, Trust Agreements, Etc.**

☐ Living will _____

☐ Powers of attorney

   ☐ Durable power of attorney for financial management _____

   ☐ Durable power of attorney for health care _____

   ☐ Other powers of attorney _____

☐ Trust agreement _____

☐ Will and codicils _____

☐ Other _____ _____

☐ _____ _____

**Final Wishes**

☐ Body bequeathal papers _____

☐ Cemetery deed _____

☐ Funeral prearrangement agreement _____

☐ Funeral prepayment agreement _____

☐ Mausoleum deed _____

☐ Uniform donor card _____

# Where to Find Records and Keys *(continued)*

**Safe-Deposit**
**Box**

**Other Locations**

### Final Wishes (continued)

☐ Other _____    _____

☐ _____    _____

### Miscellaneous Information

☐ Animal care information    _____

☐ Burglar alarm information    _____

☐ Child care information    _____

☐ Letters to be sent upon my
death    _____

☐ List of hiding places for
valuables    _____

☐ Property care information    _____

☐ Tax records    _____

### Keys and Combinations

☐ Keys to homes    _____

☐ Keys to other real estate    _____

☐ Keys to post office boxes    _____

Keys to safe-deposit box(es)    (See pages 111–112.)

☐ Keys to vehicles    _____

☐ Other keys    _____

☐ List of combinations to locks    _____

### Other

☐ Passcode to online service(s)    _____

☐ Cassettes    _____

☐ Computer and other electronic
media    _____

☐ Photos    _____

☐ Videos/movies    _____

☐ _____    _____

☐ _____    _____

☐ _____    _____

# Persons to Contact

## Professional Advisers

My lawyer is: _____ Phone: _____

Address: _____

_____

My accountant/tax preparer is: _____ Phone: _____

Address: _____

_____

Copies of my income tax returns are located: _____

_____

My dentist is: _____ Phone: _____

Address: _____

_____

My personal physician is: _____ Phone: _____

Address: _____

_____

My specialty physician is: _____ Phone: _____

Address: _____

_____

My specialty physician is: _____ Phone: _____

Address: _____

_____

My specialty physician is: _____ Phone: _____

Address: _____

_____

My _____ is: _____ Phone: _____
    *Profession*

Address: _____

_____

# Persons to Contact *(continued)*

## Service providers for my child(ren) and home

My child(ren)'s legal guardian is: _____ Phone: _____

Address: _____

_____

My child(ren)'s school or daycare provider is: _____ Phone: _____

Address: _____

_____

My child(ren)'s other school or daycare provider is: _____ Phone: _____

Address: _____

_____

My child(ren)'s babysitter is: _____ Phone: _____

Address: _____

_____

My child(ren)'s physician is: _____ Phone: _____

Address: _____

_____

My child(ren)'s dentist is: _____ Phone: _____

Address: _____

_____

List other service providers to contact, such as house cleaning service, gardener, security system service, pool maintenance service, rental property management company, etc.

| Name | Address | Phone | Type of Service |
|------|---------|-------|-----------------|
|  |  |  |  |
|  |  |  |  |
|  |  |  |  |
|  |  |  |  |

# Persons to Contact *(continued)*

The following people should be contacted in the event of my death:

| Name | Address | Phone | Relationship (Friend, Employer, Cousin, etc.) |
|------|---------|-------|-----------------------------------------------|
|      |         |       |                                               |
|      |         |       |                                               |
|      |         |       |                                               |
|      |         |       |                                               |
|      |         |       |                                               |
|      |         |       |                                               |
|      |         |       |                                               |
|      |         |       |                                               |
|      |         |       |                                               |
|      |         |       |                                               |
|      |         |       |                                               |
|      |         |       |                                               |
|      |         |       |                                               |
|      |         |       |                                               |

# CHAPTER 2

# Sharing My Personal History

No one knows your personal history as well as you do. Do your children know where you were born? Where you went to school? In what cities you have lived? Your mother's family name? Where your parents lived or are buried? The different types of work experiences you have had? The hobbies and clubs you have enjoyed through the years? Probably not.

And yet, haven't you asked yourself many of these questions in regard to your own parents? Or your grandparents? Or your brothers and sisters? Most of us become more interested in family history as we age, but if someone does not record the facts of that history for us, they will be lost. *You* are the one who can do this best for your heirs.

Go through the forms in Chapter 2 and fill in as many answers as you can. There will be many blanks when you finish. Make gathering the rest of the answers an enjoyable project. Telephone, drop a note, or e-mail your parent, brother, sister, aunt, uncle, son, or daughter and gradually complete your personal history. As a bonus, you might even rekindle family ties!

## FORMS ON MY PERSONAL HISTORY

The forms in Chapter 2 are set out in the following order:

My Family History
General Summary
Marital Background
Children
Parents
Grandparents
Brothers and Sisters

My Family Medical History
My Residences
My Educational Background
My Work Background
My Religion, Politics, and Hobbies
My Organizations, Unions, Clubs
Miscellaneous

The form entitled "General Summary" provides a place for you to record pertinent facts of your life.

Forms are provided for three spouses, six children, and five siblings. As mentioned previously, feel free to modify the forms to suit your needs. For example, if you are unmarried but have someone significant you would like to include, simply cross through *spouse* and replace it with the term you prefer to describe your relationship, such as *lifetime partner* or *special friend*. Excess forms may be removed from the book, keeping in mind that families change in unforseen ways as a result of births, deaths, divorces, and marriages.

Many of the forms have space for you to write personal notes about your relatives. Use the space as you wish. For example, you can give a brief history, explain their beliefs or accomplishments, or share personal reminiscences.

By completing the form entitled "My Family Medical History," you will be sharing information that may prove valuable in the diagnosis, early treatment, and, in some cases, prevention of certain hereditary medical conditions.

The remaining forms in Chapter 2 seek more detailed information about you—your educational background, where you have lived and worked, organizations you have joined, and your religion, politics, and hobbies.

Finally, you will find a form entitled "Miscellaneous." This is for *you* to fill in with personal notes about yourself or your family—your interests, accomplishments, thoughts, or desires. Add anything you consider to be of interest to your family and heirs. Don't be modest! If you did something in your lifetime of which you are proud, tell them about it. They will be proud, too. If something very humorous happened to you, your heirs will enjoy it. Remember how you were fascinated with the interesting stories told to you by your mother, father, and grandparents? Your heirs are just as interested in your remembrances.

A primary purpose of the forms in Chapter 2 is to provide enjoyment for your heirs. However, there are other purposes. At the time of death, some of this information can be used in the preparation of a death certificate, newspaper obituary, federal estate tax return, state inheritance tax return, income tax return, and many other administrative forms.

# BIRTH AND MARRIAGE CERTIFICATES

The vast majority of births, deaths, and marriages are reported to the proper authorities to maintain a lasting record. However, for a number of reasons, your heirs may have great difficulty obtaining these records when needed. For example, in the not too distant past, many births occurred in private homes and went unreported. Occasionally, fire destroyed courthouses or other record depositories. Records escaping this fate may be incorrect because of typographical errors, misunderstanding of names, and other errors.

There may be a long delay after a request for copies of certificates while records are corrected or reestablished. It is a good idea to request them now so they will always be on hand.

Obtain and keep in a safe-deposit box two *certified* copies each of your birth certificate, your spouse's birth certificate, your marriage certificate, and the birth certificates of your dependent children.

Each state has its own method of maintaining these records. They can usually be obtained from the county clerk, registrar, or recorder of the county in which the birth or marriage took place. Many states have a central clearing house for this at the state capital, generally called the Department of Vital Statistics.

There is no standard fee for providing these records. Fees generally range from $2 to $20. Additional copies may be available at reduced rates.

To expedite the sometimes lengthy procedure of obtaining the certificates you need, first inquire about how much each one will cost. Include a self-addressed, stamped envelope with your price request. Once you know the cost, you can write for the copies you need, enclosing the necessary payment. Use a money order or bank check, rather than your personal check, for prompt service.

Many states will not issue copies of birth or marriage certificates unless the requestor is closely related to the person named in the certificate. Therefore, it is important to identify yourself as spouse, mother, or father.

# DECREES AND JUDGMENTS OF DIVORCE AND ANNULMENT

You might need certified copies of judgments of divorce or annulment for Social Security benefits, veterans benefits, and private pension plans. You can obtain them from the clerk or registrar of the court that granted the divorce or annulment. Once again, the fee for obtaining copies varies in each state and may also depend upon the number of pages in the document.

Write a letter to the court that granted the decree or judgment to inquire about the cost of obtaining a copy of the document. Note the date and year the divorce or annulment was granted, and be sure to enclose a self-addressed, stamped envelope.

# My Family History

**Children**

**My Full Name**
Date        Place
Born
Died

**Spouse(s)**
Married
Married
Married

**Brothers & Sisters**

1.

2. **Father**
Date        Place
Born
Married
Died

3. **Mother**
Date        Place
Born
Married
Died

4. **Paternal Grandfather**
Date        Place
Born
Married
Died

5. **Paternal Grandmother**
Date        Place
Born
Married
Died

6. **Maternal Grandfather**
Date        Place
Born
Married
Died

7. **Maternal Grandmother**
Date        Place
Born
Married
Died

8. **Great Grandfather**
Born
Married
Died

9. **Great Grandmother**
Born
Married
Died

10. **Great Grandfather**
Born
Married
Died

11. **Great Grandmother**
Born
Married
Died

12. **Great Grandfather**
Born
Married
Died

13. **Great Grandmother**
Born
Married
Died

14. **Great Grandfather**
Born
Married
Died

15. **Great Grandmother**
Born
Married
Died

16. Gt. Gt. Grandfather
17. Gt. Gt. Grandmother
18. Gt. Gt. Grandfather
19. Gt. Gt. Grandmother
20. Gt. Gt. Grandfather
21. Gt. Gt. Grandmother
22. Gt. Gt. Grandfather
23. Gt. Gt. Grandmother
24. Gt. Gt. Grandfather
25. Gt. Gt. Grandmother
26. Gt. Gt. Grandfather
27. Gt. Gt. Grandmother
28. Gt. Gt. Grandfather
29. Gt. Gt. Grandmother
30. Gt. Gt. Grandfather
31. Gt. Gt. Grandmother

# General Summary

## My Personal History

My full name at present: _____
<br>First                        *Middle*              *Last*

My full name at birth: _____
<br>*First*        *Middle*        *Last*

Place of birth: _____
<br>*City*    *County*    *State*    *Country*

Date of birth: _____ Social Security #: _____

My legal name was changed to: _____
<br>*First*    *Middle*    *Last*

on: _____ by: _____
<br>*Date*    *Name of court*

located at: _____
<br>*City*    *State*

My present address: _____
<br>*Street address and apartment number*

_____ _____
<br>*Telephone #*    *City*    *State*    *ZIP code*

Year residence established in this state: _____ this community: _____

My usual occupation: _____ Industry: _____

I am a citizen of: _____ ☐ by birth  or  ☐ by naturalization

I was naturalized on: _____ at _____
<br>*Date*    *Place*

Naturalization #: _____

Military veteran: ☐ Yes ☐ No  Branch of service: _____

Dates of service: _____ Serial #: _____ Final rank: _____

Marital status: ☐ Never married ☐ Married ☐ Divorced ☐ Widowed

❖❖❖❖❖❖

My driver's license #: _____ Expires: _____

Passport number: _____ Date of issue: _____

Country of issue: _____ Location: _____

# General Summary *(continued)*

## My Personal History

Marriages
*Sp=Spouse*

|  | Full Name of Spouse at Birth | Last Name at Present or at Death | Date of Birth | Death |
|---|---|---|---|---|
| Sp #1 |  |  |  |  |
| Sp #2 |  |  |  |  |
| Sp #3 |  |  |  |  |

*(See pages 18–23 for further information about my spouses.)*

Children
*Ch=Child*

|  | Full Name of Child at Birth | Last Name at Present or at Death | Date of Birth | Death |
|---|---|---|---|---|
| Ch #1 |  |  |  |  |
| Ch #2 |  |  |  |  |
| Ch #3 |  |  |  |  |
| Ch #4 |  |  |  |  |
| Ch #5 |  |  |  |  |
| Ch #6 |  |  |  |  |

*(See pages 24–47 for further information about my children.)*

Brothers and Sisters (Siblings)
*Si=Sibling*

|  | Full Name of Brother or Sister at Birth | Last Name at Present or at Death | Date of Birth | Death |
|---|---|---|---|---|
| Si #1 |  |  |  |  |
| Si #2 |  |  |  |  |
| Si #3 |  |  |  |  |
| Si #4 |  |  |  |  |
| Si #5 |  |  |  |  |

*(See pages 58–67 for further information about my brothers and sisters.)*

# Marital Background

## My First Spouse

Full name at present: _____
First                          Middle                          Last

Full name at birth: _____
First                          Middle                          Last

Place of birth: _____
City                    County                    State                    Country

Date of birth: _____ Social Security #: _____

Citizen of _____ ☐ by birth   or   ☐ by naturalization

Date of marriage: _____ Place of marriage: _____

Present address: _____
Street address and apartment number

_____ _____ _____
Telephone #     City                              State                              ZIP code

Date of death: _____ Cause of death: _____

He/she was buried at: _____ Lot #: _____
Name of cemetery

_____
City                              State

Or:   He/she was cremated and the ashes were: _____

Or:   He/she donated his/her body to: _____
Name of medical school

We were divorced on: _____ at: _____
Date                          City                              State

We had the following children:

|     | Date of Birth | Full Name at Birth | Present Last Name |
|-----|---------------|--------------------|--------------------|
| #1  |               |                    |                    |
| #2  |               |                    |                    |
| #3  |               |                    |                    |
| #4  |               |                    |                    |
| #5  |               |                    |                    |
| #6  |               |                    |                    |

# Marital Background (continued)

## My First Spouse

_____

_____

_____

_____

_____

_____

_____

_____

_____

_____

_____

_____

_____

_____

_____

_____

_____

_____

_____

_____

_____

_____

_____

_____

_____

_____

_____

# Marital Background *(continued)*

## My Second Spouse

Full name at present: _____
First                     Middle                     Last

Full name at birth: _____
First                     Middle                     Last

Place of birth: _____
City            County            State            Country

Date of birth: _____    Social Security #: _____

Citizen of _____    ☐ by birth    or    ☐ by naturalization

Date of marriage: _____    Place of marriage: _____

Present address: _____
Street address and apartment number

_____
Telephone #    City                     State                     ZIP code

Date of death: _____    Cause of death: _____

He/she was buried at: _____    Lot #: _____
Name of cemetery

_____
City                     State

*Or:*   He/she was cremated and the ashes were: _____

*Or:*   He/she donated his/her body to: _____
Name of medical school

We were divorced on: _____    at: _____
Date                     City                     State

We had the following children:

|     | Date of Birth | Full Name at Birth | Present Last Name |
|-----|---------------|--------------------|--------------------|
| #1  |               |                    |                    |
| #2  |               |                    |                    |
| #3  |               |                    |                    |
| #4  |               |                    |                    |
| #5  |               |                    |                    |
| #6  |               |                    |                    |

# Marital Background *(continued)*

## My Second Spouse

_____

_____

_____

_____

_____

_____

_____

_____

_____

_____

_____

_____

_____

_____

_____

_____

_____

_____

_____

_____

_____

_____

_____

_____

_____

# Marital Background *(continued)*

## My Third Spouse

Full name at present: _____
          First                    Middle                    Last

Full name at birth: _____
          First                    Middle                    Last

Place of birth: _____
          City              County              State              Country

Date of birth: _____ Social Security #: _____

Citizen of _____ ☐ by birth  or  ☐ by naturalization

Date of marriage: _____ Place of marriage: _____

Present address: _____
          Street address and apartment number

_____ _____
Telephone #     City                         State                    ZIP code

Date of death: _____ Cause of death: _____

He/she was buried at: _____ Lot #: _____
          Name of cemetery

_____
          City                         State

*Or:*  He/she was cremated and the ashes were: _____

*Or:*  He/she donated his/her body to: _____
                                        Name of medical school

We were divorced on: _____ at: _____
          Date                         City                    State

We had the following children:

|     | Date of Birth | Full Name at Birth | Present Last Name |
|-----|---------------|--------------------|--------------------|
| #1  |               |                    |                    |
| #2  |               |                    |                    |
| #3  |               |                    |                    |
| #4  |               |                    |                    |
| #5  |               |                    |                    |
| #6  |               |                    |                    |

# Marital Background *(continued)*

## My Third Spouse

_____

_____

_____

_____

_____

_____

_____

_____

_____

_____

_____

_____

_____

_____

_____

_____

_____

_____

_____

_____

_____

_____

_____

_____

_____

_____

_____

# Children

## My First Child

Child's full name at present: _____
First               Middle               Last

Child's full name at birth: _____
First               Middle               Last

Child's other parent: _____  _____
First          Middle          Last          Phone #

Other parent's address: _____

Date of birth: _____ Place of birth: _____
City          County          State          Country

Adopted? _____ (If so, give details on next page.)  Social Security #: _____

Citizen of: _____  ☐ by birth  or  ☐ by naturalization

Present address: _____
Street address and apartment number

_____  _____  _____  _____
Telephone #        City                              State             ZIP code

Date of death: _____ Cause of death: _____

Child is buried at: _____  Lot #: _____
Name of cemetery

_____  _____
City                                              State

*Or:*  Child was cremated and the ashes were: _____

*Or:*  Child donated body to: _____
Name of medical school

☐ Child has never married.

☐ Child has been married _____ times. The names of the child's spouses, marriage dates, etc., are as follows:

|     | Name of Spouse (Before Marriage) | Date of Birth | Date of Marriage | Date of Death | Divorce |
|-----|----------------------------------|---------------|------------------|---------------|---------|
| #1  |                                  |               |                  |               |         |
| #2  |                                  |               |                  |               |         |
| #3  |                                  |               |                  |               |         |

# Children *(continued)*

## My First Child

_____

_____

_____

_____

_____

_____

_____

_____

_____

_____

_____

_____

_____

_____

_____

_____

_____

_____

_____

_____

_____

_____

_____

_____

_____

# Children *(continued)*

## My First Child's Children

Child's full name at present: _____

☐ Never had any children.

☐ Had _____ children.

*Gch = Grandchild*

| | Full Name of My Grandchild at Birth | Last Name at Present or at Death | Date of Birth | Death |
|---|---|---|---|---|
| Gch #1 | | | | |
| Gch #2 | | | | |
| Gch #3 | | | | |
| Gch #4 | | | | |
| Gch #5 | | | | |
| Gch #6 | | | | |

| | Name of My Grandchild's Present Spouse | Address |
|---|---|---|
| Gch #1 | | |
| Gch #2 | | |
| Gch #3 | | |
| Gch #4 | | |
| Gch #5 | | |
| Gch #6 | | |

# Children (continued)

## My First Child's Children

---
---
---
---
---
---
---
---
---
---
---
---
---
---
---
---
---
---
---
---
---
---
---
---
---
---
---

# Children *(continued)*

## My Second Child

Child's full name at present: _____
First                    Middle                Last

Child's full name at birth: _____
First                   Middle                Last

Child's other parent: _____ _____
First        Middle        Last        Phone #

Other parent's address: _____

Date of birth: _____  Place of birth: _____
City      County      State      Country

Adopted? _____ (If so, give details on next page.)  Social Security #: _____

Citizen of: _____ ☐ by birth  or  ☐ by naturalization

Present address: _____
Street address and apartment number

_____  _____
Telephone #    City                    State        ZIP code

Date of death: _____  Cause of death: _____

Child is buried at: _____  Lot #: _____
Name of cemetery

_____
City                      State

*Or:*  Child was cremated and the ashes were: _____

*Or:*  Child donated body to: _____
Name of medical school

☐ Child has never married.

☐ Child has been married _____ times. The names of the child's spouses, marriage dates, etc., are as follows:

|  | Name of Spouse (Before Marriage) | Date of Birth | Date of Marriage | Date of Death | Divorce |
|---|---|---|---|---|---|
| #1 |  |  |  |  |  |
| #2 |  |  |  |  |  |
| #3 |  |  |  |  |  |

# Children *(continued)*

## My Second Child

_____

_____

_____

_____

_____

_____

_____

_____

_____

_____

_____

_____

_____

_____

_____

_____

_____

_____

_____

_____

_____

_____

_____

_____

_____

_____

# Children *(continued)*

## My Second Child's Children

Child's full name at present: _____

☐ Never had any children.

☐ Had _____ children.

*Gch = Grandchild*

|  | Full Name of My Grandchild at Birth | Last Name at Present or at Death | Date of Birth | Death |
|---|---|---|---|---|
| Gch #1 |  |  |  |  |
| Gch #2 |  |  |  |  |
| Gch #3 |  |  |  |  |
| Gch #4 |  |  |  |  |
| Gch #5 |  |  |  |  |
| Gch #6 |  |  |  |  |

|  | Name of My Grandchild's Present Spouse | Address |
|---|---|---|
| Gch #1 |  |  |
| Gch #2 |  |  |
| Gch #3 |  |  |
| Gch #4 |  |  |
| Gch #5 |  |  |
| Gch #6 |  |  |

# Children *(continued)*

## My Second Child's Children

_____

_____

_____

_____

_____

_____

_____

_____

_____

_____

_____

_____

_____

_____

_____

_____

_____

_____

_____

_____

_____

_____

_____

_____

_____

_____

_____

# Children *(continued)*

## My Third Child

Child's full name at present: _____
First                          Middle                          Last

Child's full name at birth: _____
First                          Middle                          Last

Child's other parent: _____  _____
First              Middle              Last                Phone #

Other parent's address: _____

Date of birth: _____ Place of birth: _____
City              County              State              Country

Adopted? _____ (If so, give details on next page.)  Social Security #: _____

Citizen of: _____  ☐ by birth  or  ☐ by naturalization

Present address: _____
Street address and apartment number

_____  _____
Telephone #      City                              State                  ZIP code

Date of death: _____ Cause of death: _____

Child is buried at: _____ Lot #: _____
Name of cemetery

_____
City                                          State

*Or:*  Child was cremated and the ashes were: _____

*Or:*  Child donated body to: _____
Name of medical school

☐ Child has never married.

☐ Child has been married _____ times. The names of the child's spouses, marriage dates, etc., are as follows:

|     | Name of Spouse (Before Marriage) | Date of Birth | Date of Marriage | Date of Death | Divorce |
|-----|----------------------------------|---------------|------------------|---------------|---------|
| #1  |                                  |               |                  |               |         |
| #2  |                                  |               |                  |               |         |
| #3  |                                  |               |                  |               |         |

# Children *(continued)*

## My Third Child

_____

_____

_____

_____

_____

_____

_____

_____

_____

_____

_____

_____

_____

_____

_____

_____

_____

_____

_____

_____

_____

_____

_____

_____

# Children *(continued)*

## My Third Child's Children

Child's full name at present: _____

☐ Never had any children.

☐ Had _____ children.

*Gch = Grandchild*

| | Full Name of My Grandchild at Birth | Last Name at Present or at Death | Date of | |
|---|---|---|---|---|
| | | | Birth | Death |
| Gch #1 | | | | |
| Gch #2 | | | | |
| Gch #3 | | | | |
| Gch #4 | | | | |
| Gch #5 | | | | |
| Gch #6 | | | | |

| | Name of My Grandchild's Present Spouse | Address |
|---|---|---|
| Gch #1 | | |
| Gch #2 | | |
| Gch #3 | | |
| Gch #4 | | |
| Gch #5 | | |
| Gch #6 | | |

# Children (continued)

## My Third Child's Children

_____

_____

_____

_____

_____

_____

_____

_____

_____

_____

_____

_____

_____

_____

_____

_____

_____

_____

_____

_____

_____

_____

_____

_____

_____

# Children *(continued)*

## My Fourth Child

Child's full name at present: _____
<br>First          Middle          Last

Child's full name at birth: _____
<br>First          Middle          Last

Child's other parent: _____  _____
<br>First     Middle     Last     Phone #

Other parent's address: _____

Date of birth: _____ Place of birth: _____
<br>City     County     State     Country

Adopted? _____ (If so, give details on next page.)  Social Security #: _____

Citizen of: _____ ☐ by birth   or   ☐ by naturalization

Present address: _____
<br>Street address and apartment number

_____  _____
<br>Telephone #     City     State     ZIP code

Date of death: _____ Cause of death: _____

Child is buried at: _____ Lot #: _____
<br>Name of cemetery

_____
<br>City     State

*Or:*   Child was cremated and the ashes were: _____

*Or:*   Child donated body to: _____
<br>Name of medical school

☐ Child has never married.

☐ Child has been married _____ times. The names of the child's spouses, marriage dates, etc., are as follows:

| | Name of Spouse (Before Marriage) | Date of Birth | Date of Marriage | Date of Death | Date of Divorce |
|---|---|---|---|---|---|
| #1 | | | | | |
| #2 | | | | | |
| #3 | | | | | |

# Children (continued)

## My Fourth Child

_____

_____

_____

_____

_____

_____

_____

_____

_____

_____

_____

_____

_____

_____

_____

_____

_____

_____

_____

_____

_____

_____

_____

_____

_____

# Children *(continued)*

## My Fourth Child's Children

Child's full name at present: _____

☐ Never had any children.

☐ Had _____ children.

*Gch = Grandchild*

|  | Full Name of My Grandchild at Birth | Last Name at Present or at Death | Date of Birth | Date of Death |
|---|---|---|---|---|
| Gch #1 |  |  |  |  |
| Gch #2 |  |  |  |  |
| Gch #3 |  |  |  |  |
| Gch #4 |  |  |  |  |
| Gch #5 |  |  |  |  |
| Gch #6 |  |  |  |  |

|  | Name of My Grandchild's Present Spouse | Address |
|---|---|---|
| Gch #1 |  |  |
| Gch #2 |  |  |
| Gch #3 |  |  |
| Gch #4 |  |  |
| Gch #5 |  |  |
| Gch #6 |  |  |

# Children *(continued)*

## My Fourth Child's Children

_____

_____

_____

_____

_____

_____

_____

_____

_____

_____

_____

_____

_____

_____

_____

_____

_____

_____

_____

_____

_____

_____

_____

_____

_____

# Children *(continued)*

## My Fifth Child

Child's full name at present: _____
<br>First      Middle      Last

Child's full name at birth: _____
<br>First      Middle      Last

Child's other parent: _____ _____
<br>First   Middle   Last   Phone #

Other parent's address: _____

Date of birth: _____ Place of birth: _____
<br>City   County   State   Country

Adopted? _____ (If so, give details on next page.)  Social Security #: _____

Citizen of: _____  ☐ by birth  or  ☐ by naturalization

Present address: _____
<br>Street address and apartment number

_____ _____
<br>Telephone # City     State    ZIP code

Date of death: _____ Cause of death: _____

Child is buried at: _____ Lot #: _____
<br>Name of cemetery

_____
<br>City         State

*Or:*  Child was cremated and the ashes were: _____

*Or:*  Child donated body to: _____
<br>Name of medical school

☐ Child has never married.

☐ Child has been married _____ times. The names of the child's spouses, marriage dates, etc., are as follows:

| | Name of Spouse (Before Marriage) | Date of Birth | Date of Marriage | Date of Death | Divorce |
|---|---|---|---|---|---|
| #1 | | | | | |
| #2 | | | | | |
| #3 | | | | | |

# Children (continued)

## My Fifth Child

_____

_____

_____

_____

_____

_____

_____

_____

_____

_____

_____

_____

_____

_____

_____

_____

_____

_____

_____

_____

_____

_____

_____

_____

# Children *(continued)*

## My Fifth Child's Children

Child's full name at present: _____

☐ Never had any children.

☐ Had _____ children.

*Gch = Grandchild*

|  | Full Name of My Grandchild at Birth | Last Name at Present or at Death | Date of Birth | Death |
|---|---|---|---|---|
| Gch #1 |  |  |  |  |
| Gch #2 |  |  |  |  |
| Gch #3 |  |  |  |  |
| Gch #4 |  |  |  |  |
| Gch #5 |  |  |  |  |
| Gch #6 |  |  |  |  |

|  | Name of My Grandchild's Present Spouse | Address |
|---|---|---|
| Gch #1 |  |  |
| Gch #2 |  |  |
| Gch #3 |  |  |
| Gch #4 |  |  |
| Gch #5 |  |  |
| Gch #6 |  |  |

# Children *(continued)*

## My Fifth Child's Children

_____

_____

_____

_____

_____

_____

_____

_____

_____

_____

_____

_____

_____

_____

_____

_____

_____

_____

_____

_____

_____

_____

_____

_____

_____

_____

# Children *(continued)*

## My Sixth Child

Child's full name at present: _____
<br>First           *First*           *Middle*           *Last*

Child's full name at birth: _____
<br>*First*           *Middle*           *Last*

Child's other parent: _____   _____
<br>*First*     *Middle*     *Last*     *Phone #*

Other parent's address: _____

Date of birth: _____ Place of birth: _____
<br>*City*     *County*     *State*     *Country*

Adopted? _____ (If so, give details on next page.) Social Security #: _____

Citizen of: _____ ☐ by birth  or  ☐ by naturalization

Present address: _____
<br>*Street address and apartment number*

_____   _____
<br>*Telephone #*     *City*     *State*     *ZIP code*

Date of death: _____ Cause of death: _____

Child is buried at: _____ Lot #: _____
<br>*Name of cemetery*

_____
<br>*City*     *State*

*Or:*  Child was cremated and the ashes were: _____

*Or:*  Child donated body to: _____
<br>*Name of medical school*

☐ Child has never married.

☐ Child has been married _____ times. The names of the child's spouses, marriage dates, etc., are as follows:

| | Name of Spouse (Before Marriage) | Date of Birth | Date of Marriage | Date of Death | Divorce |
|---|---|---|---|---|---|
| #1 | | | | | |
| #2 | | | | | |
| #3 | | | | | |

# Children (continued)

## My Sixth Child

_____

_____

_____

_____

_____

_____

_____

_____

_____

_____

_____

_____

_____

_____

_____

_____

_____

_____

_____

_____

_____

_____

_____

_____

_____

# Children *(continued)*

## My Sixth Child's Children

Child's full name at present: _____

☐ Never had any children.

☐ Had _____ children.

*Gch = Grandchild*

|  | Full Name of My Grandchild at Birth | Last Name at Present or at Death | Date of Birth | Death |
|---|---|---|---|---|
| Gch #1 |  |  |  |  |
| Gch #2 |  |  |  |  |
| Gch #3 |  |  |  |  |
| Gch #4 |  |  |  |  |
| Gch #5 |  |  |  |  |
| Gch #6 |  |  |  |  |

|  | Name of My Grandchild's Present Spouse | Address |
|---|---|---|
| Gch #1 |  |  |
| Gch #2 |  |  |
| Gch #3 |  |  |
| Gch #4 |  |  |
| Gch #5 |  |  |
| Gch #6 |  |  |

# Children (continued)

## My Sixth Child's Children

_____

_____

_____

_____

_____

_____

_____

_____

_____

_____

_____

_____

_____

_____

_____

_____

_____

_____

_____

_____

_____

_____

_____

# Parents

## Father

Full name at present: _____
                         *First*               *Middle*            *Last*

Full name at birth: _____
                  *First*             *Middle*          *Last*

Place of birth: _____
            *City*        *County*       *State*       *Country*

Date of birth: _____

Present address: _____
      *Street address and apartment number*

_____    _____
*Telephone #*    *City*                *State*         *ZIP code*

Date of death: _____    Cause of death: _____

Buried at: _____    Lot #: _____
     *Name of cemetery*

_____
*City*                         *State*

*Or:*   Cremated and ashes were: _____

_____

*Or:*   Donated body to: _____
                   *Name of medical school*

My parents were married on: _____    at: _____

_____
            *City*                    *State*

My parents were divorced on: _____    at: _____
                       *Date*        *City*      *State*

☐ My father never married.

☐ My father married _____ times.

| | Name of Spouse (Before Marriage) | Date of Marriage | Date of Death | Date of Divorce |
|---|---|---|---|---|
| #1 | | | | |
| #2 | | | | |
| #3 | | | | |

# Parents (continued)

## Father

_____

_____

_____

_____

_____

_____

_____

_____

_____

_____

_____

_____

_____

_____

_____

_____

_____

_____

_____

_____

_____

_____

_____

_____

# Parents *(continued)*

## Mother

Full name at present: _____
                                                  First                        Middle                        Last

Full name at birth: _____
                                            First                        Middle                        Last

Place of birth: _____
                                    City                  County                  State                  Country

Date of birth: _____

Present address: _____
                        *Street address and apartment number*

_____    _____
*Telephone #*        *City*                                        *State*                        *ZIP code*

Date of death: _____    Cause of death: _____

Buried at: _____    Lot #: _____
                *Name of cemetery*

_____
*City*                                            *State*

*Or:*    Cremated and ashes were: _____

_____

*Or:*    Donated body to: _____
                                        *Name of medical school*

My parents were married on: _____    at: _____

_____
                        *City*                                            *State*

My parents were divorced on: _____    at: _____
                                                *Date*                      *City*              *State*

☐ My mother never married.

☐ My mother married _____ times.

| | Name of Spouse (Before Marriage) | Date of Marriage | Date of Death | Date of Divorce |
|---|---|---|---|---|
| #1 | | | | |
| #2 | | | | |
| #3 | | | | |

# Parents *(continued)*

## Mother

_____

_____

_____

_____

_____

_____

_____

_____

_____

_____

_____

_____

_____

_____

_____

_____

_____

_____

_____

_____

_____

_____

_____

# Grandparents

## My Father's Parents

My grandparents were married on: _____ at: _____

_____
                 *City*                                        *State*

My grandparents were divorced on: _____ at:_____
                                           *Date*               *City*               *State*

☐ My grandparents never married.

❖❖❖❖❖❖

### GRANDFATHER

My grandfather's full name at birth: _____
                                          *First*            *Middle*            *Last*

Place of birth: _____
                *City*         *County*         *State*        *Country*

Citizen of: _____ ☐ by birth or ☐ by naturalization

Date of birth: _____ Date of death: _____

My grandfather is buried at: _____ Lot #: _____
                                *Name of cemetery*

_____
                 *City*                                          *State*

*Or:* My grandfather was cremated and his ashes were: _____

*Or:* My grandfather donated his body to: _____
                                        *Name of medical school*

☐ My grandfather married _____ times.

☐ My grandfather never married.

| | Name of Wife (Before Marriage) | Date of Marriage | Date of Death | Date of Divorce |
|----|-------------------------------|------------------|---------------|-----------------|
| #1 | | | | |
| #2 | | | | |
| #3 | | | | |

# Grandparents *(continued)*

## My Father's Parents

### GRANDMOTHER

My grandmother's full name at birth: _____
First　　　　　　Middle　　　　　　Last

Place of birth: _____
City　　　　　County　　　　　State　　　　　Country

Citizen of: _____ ☐ by birth　or　☐ by naturalization

Date of birth: _____ Date of death: _____

My grandmother is buried at: _____ Lot #: _____
Name of cemetery

_____
City　　　　　　　　　　　State

*Or:* My grandmother was cremated and her ashes were: _____

*Or:* My grandmother donated her body to: _____
Name of medical school

☐ My grandmother married _____ times.

☐ My grandmother never married.

|  | Name of Husband | Date of Marriage | Date of Death | Date of Divorce |
|---|---|---|---|---|
| #1 |  |  |  |  |
| #2 |  |  |  |  |
| #3 |  |  |  |  |

# Grandparents *(continued)*

## My Father's Parents

_____

_____

_____

_____

_____

_____

_____

_____

_____

_____

_____

_____

_____

_____

_____

_____

_____

_____

_____

_____

_____

_____

_____

_____

# Grandparents *(continued)*

## My Mother's Parents

My grandparents were married on: _____ at: _____

_____
　　　　　　　　　　　　*City*　　　　　　　　　　　　　　　　　　　　*State*

My grandparents were divorced on: _____ at:_____
　　　　　　　　　　　　　　　　　　*Date*　　　　　　　　*City*　　　　　　*State*

☐ My grandparents never married.

❖❖❖❖❖❖

### GRANDFATHER

My grandfather's full name at birth: _____
　　　　　　　　　　　　　　　　　　*First*　　　　　　*Middle*　　　　　*Last*

Place of birth: _____
　　　　　　　　*City*　　　　　*County*　　　　　*State*　　　　　*Country*

Citizen of: _____ ☐ by birth  or  ☐ by naturalization

Date of birth: _____ Date of death: _____

My grandfather is buried at: _____ Lot #: _____
　　　　　　　　　　　　　*Name of cemetery*

_____
　　　　　　　　*City*　　　　　　　　　　　　　　　　　　*State*

*Or:*  My grandfather was cremated and his ashes were: _____

*Or:*  My grandfather donated his body to: _____
　　　　　　　　　　　　　　　　　　　　　　　*Name of medical school*

☐ My grandfather married _____ times.

☐ My grandfather never married.

| | Name of Wife (Before Marriage) | Date of Marriage | Date of | |
| --- | --- | --- | --- | --- |
| | | | Death | Divorce |
| #1 | | | | |
| #2 | | | | |
| #3 | | | | |

# Grandparents *(continued)*

## My Mother's Parents

### GRANDMOTHER

My grandmother's full name at birth: _____
First                    Middle                    Last

Place of birth: _____
City                County                State                Country

Citizen of: _____   ☐ by birth   or   ☐ by naturalization

Date of birth: _____   Date of death: _____

My grandmother is buried at: _____   Lot #: _____
Name of cemetery

_____
City                                        State

*Or:*   My grandmother was cremated and her ashes were: _____

*Or:*   My grandmother donated her body to: _____
Name of medical school

☐ My grandmother married _____ times.

☐ My grandmother never married.

| | Name of Husband | Date of Marriage | Date of Death | Date of Divorce |
|---|---|---|---|---|
| #1 | | | | |
| #2 | | | | |
| #3 | | | | |

# Grandparents *(continued)*

## My Mother's Parents

_____

_____

_____

_____

_____

_____

_____

_____

_____

_____

_____

_____

_____

_____

_____

_____

_____

_____

_____

_____

_____

_____

_____

_____

# Brothers and Sisters

## My First Sibling

Full name at present: _____
First                          Middle                          Last

Full name at birth: _____
First                          Middle                          Last

Place of birth: _____
City                    County                   State                   Country

Citizen of: _____    ☐ by birth   or   ☐ by naturalization

Date of birth: _____    Date of death: _____

This sibling is related to me by:    ☐ full blood          ☐ half blood          ☐ adoption
(common parents)         (one common parent)

If related by half blood, or adopted, sibling's parents (or adopting parents) were:

Mother: _____    Father: _____

Sibling's present address: _____
Street address and apartment number

_____    _____
Telephone #                 City                                State                        ZIP code

Sibling is buried at: _____    Lot #: _____
Name of cemetery

_____
City                                                    State

☐ Sibling has never married.    ☐ Sibling has been married _____ times.

|     | Name of Spouse (Before Marriage) | Date of Marriage | Date of Death | Divorce |
| --- | --- | --- | --- | --- |
| #1  |     |     |     |     |
| #2  |     |     |     |     |
| #3  |     |     |     |     |

☐ Sibling has had _____ children born alive or adopted; or ☐ sibling has never had any children.

|     | Full Name of Child at Birth (My Nieces and Nephews) | Last Name at Present or at Death | Date of Birth | Death |
| --- | --- | --- | --- | --- |
| #1  |     |     |     |     |
| #2  |     |     |     |     |
| #3  |     |     |     |     |
| #4  |     |     |     |     |
| #5  |     |     |     |     |
| #6  |     |     |     |     |

# Brothers and Sisters (continued)

## My First Sibling

_____

_____

_____

_____

_____

_____

_____

_____

_____

_____

_____

_____

_____

_____

_____

_____

_____

_____

_____

_____

_____

_____

_____

_____

_____

# Brothers and Sisters *(continued)*

## My Second Sibling

Full name at present: _____
First                          Middle                           Last

Full name at birth: _____
First                          Middle                           Last

Place of birth: _____
City                    County                    State                    Country

Citizen of: _____ ☐ by birth   or   ☐ by naturalization

Date of birth: _____ Date of death: _____

This sibling is related to me by:   ☐ full blood            ☐ half blood                ☐ adoption
(common parents)          (one common parent)

If related by half blood, or adopted, sibling's parents (or adopting parents) were:

Mother: _____ Father: _____

Sibling's present address: _____
Street address and apartment number

_____
Telephone #              City                              State                    ZIP code

Sibling is buried at: _____ Lot #: _____
Name of cemetery

_____
City                                              State

☐ Sibling has never married.   ☐ Sibling has been married _____ times.

|    | Name of Spouse (Before Marriage) | Date of Marriage | Date of Death | Divorce |
|----|----------------------------------|------------------|---------------|---------|
| #1 |                                  |                  |               |         |
| #2 |                                  |                  |               |         |
| #3 |                                  |                  |               |         |

☐ Sibling has had _____ children born alive or adopted; or ☐ sibling has never had any children.

|    | Full Name of Child at Birth (My Nieces and Nephews) | Last Name at Present or at Death | Date of Birth | Death |
|----|-----------------------------------------------------|----------------------------------|---------------|-------|
| #1 |                                                     |                                  |               |       |
| #2 |                                                     |                                  |               |       |
| #3 |                                                     |                                  |               |       |
| #4 |                                                     |                                  |               |       |
| #5 |                                                     |                                  |               |       |
| #6 |                                                     |                                  |               |       |

# Brothers and Sisters *(continued)*

## My Second Sibling

_____

_____

_____

_____

_____

_____

_____

_____

_____

_____

_____

_____

_____

_____

_____

_____

_____

_____

_____

_____

_____

_____

_____

_____

# Brothers and Sisters *(continued)*

## My Third Sibling

Full name at present: _____
First                          Middle                          Last

Full name at birth: _____
First                          Middle                          Last

Place of birth: _____
City                    County                    State                    Country

Citizen of: _____    ☐ by birth   or   ☐ by naturalization

Date of birth: _____    Date of death: _____

This sibling is related to me by:   ☐ full blood          ☐ half blood          ☐ adoption
(common parents)          (one common parent)

If related by half blood, or adopted, sibling's parents (or adopting parents) were:

Mother: _____    Father: _____

Sibling's present address: _____
Street address and apartment number

_____    _____
Telephone #              City                         State                    ZIP code

Sibling is buried at: _____    Lot #: _____
Name of cemetery

_____
City                                              State

☐ Sibling has never married.   ☐ Sibling has been married _____ times.

|    | Name of Spouse (Before Marriage) | Date of Marriage | Date of Death | Divorce |
|----|----------------------------------|------------------|---------------|---------|
| #1 |                                  |                  |               |         |
| #2 |                                  |                  |               |         |
| #3 |                                  |                  |               |         |

☐ Sibling has had _____ children born alive or adopted; or ☐ sibling has never had any children.

|    | Full Name of Child at Birth (My Nieces and Nephews) | Last Name at Present or at Death | Date of Birth | Death |
|----|-----------------------------------------------------|----------------------------------|---------------|-------|
| #1 |                                                     |                                  |               |       |
| #2 |                                                     |                                  |               |       |
| #3 |                                                     |                                  |               |       |
| #4 |                                                     |                                  |               |       |
| #5 |                                                     |                                  |               |       |
| #6 |                                                     |                                  |               |       |

# Brothers and Sisters *(continued)*

## My Third Sibling

_____

_____

_____

_____

_____

_____

_____

_____

_____

_____

_____

_____

_____

_____

_____

_____

_____

_____

_____

_____

_____

_____

_____

_____

_____

# Brothers and Sisters *(continued)*

## My Fourth Sibling

Full name at present: _____
First                    Middle                    Last

Full name at birth: _____
First                    Middle                    Last

Place of birth: _____
City                County               State                Country

Citizen of: _____    ☐ by birth   or   ☐ by naturalization

Date of birth: _____    Date of death: _____

This sibling is related to me by:   ☐ full blood          ☐ half blood          ☐ adoption
(common parents)      (one common parent)

If related by half blood, or adopted, sibling's parents (or adopting parents) were:

Mother: _____    Father: _____

Sibling's present address: _____
Street address and apartment number

_____ _____
Telephone #              City                         State              ZIP code

Sibling is buried at: _____    Lot #: _____
Name of cemetery

_____
City                                  State

☐ Sibling has never married.   ☐ Sibling has been married _____ times.

|    | Name of Spouse (Before Marriage) | Date of Marriage | Date of Death | Divorce |
|----|----------------------------------|------------------|---------------|---------|
| #1 |                                  |                  |               |         |
| #2 |                                  |                  |               |         |
| #3 |                                  |                  |               |         |

☐ Sibling has had _____ children born alive or adopted; or  ☐ sibling has never had any children.

|    | Full Name of Child at Birth (My Nieces and Nephews) | Last Name at Present or at Death | Birth | Death |
|----|------------------------------------------------------|----------------------------------|-------|-------|
| #1 |                                                      |                                  |       |       |
| #2 |                                                      |                                  |       |       |
| #3 |                                                      |                                  |       |       |
| #4 |                                                      |                                  |       |       |
| #5 |                                                      |                                  |       |       |
| #6 |                                                      |                                  |       |       |

# Brothers and Sisters (continued)

## My Fourth Sibling

_____

_____

_____

_____

_____

_____

_____

_____

_____

_____

_____

_____

_____

_____

_____

_____

_____

_____

_____

_____

_____

_____

_____

_____

_____

# Brothers and Sisters (continued)

## My Fifth Sibling

Full name at present: _____
First     Middle     Last

Full name at birth: _____
First     Middle     Last

Place of birth: _____
City    County    State    Country

Citizen of: _____ ☐ by birth   or  ☐ by naturalization

Date of birth: _____ Date of death: _____

This sibling is related to me by: ☐ full blood  ☐ half blood   ☐ adoption
          (common parents) (one common parent)

If related by half blood, or adopted, sibling's parents (or adopting parents) were:

Mother: _____  Father: _____

Sibling's present address: _____
       Street address and apartment number

_____ _____
Telephone #   City      State    ZIP code

Sibling is buried at: _____ Lot #: _____
     Name of cemetery

_____
City           State

☐ Sibling has never married.   ☐ Sibling has been married _____ times.

|  | Name of Spouse (Before Marriage) | Date of Marriage | Date of Death | Divorce |
|---|---|---|---|---|
| #1 | | | | |
| #2 | | | | |
| #3 | | | | |

☐ Sibling has had _____ children born alive or adopted; or ☐ sibling has never had any children.

|  | Full Name of Child at Birth (My Nieces and Nephews) | Last Name at Present or at Death | Date of Birth | Death |
|---|---|---|---|---|
| #1 | | | | |
| #2 | | | | |
| #3 | | | | |
| #4 | | | | |
| #5 | | | | |
| #6 | | | | |

# Brothers and Sisters (continued)

## My Fifth Sibling

# My Family Medical History

Knowledge of family medical history may help other family members with the diagnosis, early treatment, and, in some cases, prevention of hereditary medical conditions. Have you or has any blood relative had any of the following? (Include parents, grandparents, sisters, brothers, uncles, aunts, and children.)

**Yes  No**                                                                 **Who?**

☐ ☐ Alcoholism _____

☐ ☐ Alzheimer's disease _____

☐ ☐ Arthritis _____

☐ ☐ Birth defects (describe) _____ _____

☐ ☐ Blood disorder (describe, e.g., hemophilia, _____

   thalassemia) _____ _____

   Cancer: _____

☐ ☐   Breast cancer _____

☐ ☐   Colon cancer _____

☐ ☐   Melanoma _____

☐ ☐   Other cancer (describe) _____ _____

   _____ _____

☐ ☐ Chromosomal disorder (describe, e.g., Down's _____

   syndrome) _____ _____

☐ ☐ Collagen vascular disease (describe, e.g., lupus _____

   erythematosus, Raynaud's disease, rheumatoid _____

   arthritis, scleroderma) _____ _____

☐ ☐ Cystic fibrosis _____

☐ ☐ Diabetes _____

☐ ☐ Endometriosis _____

☐ ☐ Eczema _____

☐ ☐ Epilepsy (seizures) _____

☐ ☐ Glaucoma _____

☐ ☐ Gout _____

☐ ☐ Hay fever _____

   Heart disease: _____

☐ ☐   High blood pressure _____

☐ ☐   High cholesterol _____

☐ ☐   Other heart disorder (describe, e.g., Marfan _____

   syndrome) _____ _____

☐ ☐ Inflammatory bowel disease _____

☐ ☐ Kidney stones _____

☐ ☐ Lung disease _____

☐ ☐ Mental retardation _____

☐ ☐ Muscular dystrophy _____

☐ ☐ Neurological disorder (describe, e.g., Huntington's _____

   chorea, Tay-Sachs disease) _____ _____

☐ ☐ Osteoporosis _____

☐ ☐ Psoriasis _____

☐ ☐ Psychiatric disorder (describe) _____ _____

☐ ☐ Scoliosis _____

☐ ☐ Sickle cell disease or trait _____

☐ ☐ Stroke _____

☐ ☐ Thyroid disorder (describe) _____ _____

☐ ☐ Ulcers _____

☐ ☐ Other hereditary disorder(s) (describe) _____ _____

# My Residences

## Personal History

I lived in the following towns, cities, and states at the street addresses listed:

| Address | City | State | Dates |
|---|---|---|---|
|  |  |  |  |
|  |  |  |  |
|  |  |  |  |
|  |  |  |  |
|  |  |  |  |
|  |  |  |  |
|  |  |  |  |
|  |  |  |  |
|  |  |  |  |
|  |  |  |  |
|  |  |  |  |
|  |  |  |  |
|  |  |  |  |
|  |  |  |  |
|  |  |  |  |
|  |  |  |  |
|  |  |  |  |
|  |  |  |  |
|  |  |  |  |
|  |  |  |  |
|  |  |  |  |
|  |  |  |  |
|  |  |  |  |

# My Educational Background

## Personal History

I attended the following elementary schools:

| Name of School | Location | Grades Attended | Dates Attended |
|---|---|---|---|
|  |  |  |  |
|  |  |  |  |
|  |  |  |  |

I attended the following junior high schools (or middle schools):

| Name of School | Location | Grades Attended | Dates Attended |
|---|---|---|---|
|  |  |  |  |
|  |  |  |  |
|  |  |  |  |

I attended the following high schools (or preparatory schools):

| Name of School | Location | Grades Attended | Dates Attended | Graduated? |
|---|---|---|---|---|
|  |  |  |  |  |
|  |  |  |  |  |
|  |  |  |  |  |

I attended the following institutions of higher learning:

| Name of Institution | Location | Degree | Dates Attended |
|---|---|---|---|
|  |  |  |  |
|  |  |  |  |
|  |  |  |  |

# My Educational Background *(continued)*

## Personal History

I was involved in the following extracurricular activities: (List athletics, debating, drama, music, art, school newspaper, etc.)

_____

_____

_____

_____

_____

_____

_____

_____

_____

I received the following educational honors, scholarships, commendations, etc.: (List details.)

_____

_____

_____

_____

_____

_____

_____

_____

# My Work Background

## Personal History

| Names of Primary Employers (List most current first) | Location/Phone # | Dates | Type of Work |
|---|---|---|---|
| | | | |
| | | | |
| | | | |
| | | | |
| | | | |
| | | | |
| | | | |
| | | | |
| | | | |

☐ I retired from work on: _____
                              *Date*

☐ I am presently employed (describe place of employment or self-employment, type of work, etc.):

_____

_____

_____

_____

Describe any interesting facts, over the years, concerning employment:

_____

_____

_____

_____

# My Work Background *(continued)*

## Personal History

_____

_____

_____

_____

_____

_____

_____

_____

_____

_____

_____

_____

_____

_____

_____

_____

_____

_____

_____

_____

_____

_____

_____

_____

_____

# My Religion, Politics, and Hobbies

## Personal History

My religious memberships, activities, and beliefs are as follows:

_____

_____

_____

_____

_____

_____

My political memberships, activities, and beliefs are as follows:

_____

_____

_____

_____

_____

_____

Over the years, I have pursued the following hobbies:

_____

_____

_____

_____

_____

_____

# My Religion, Politics, and Hobbies (continued)

## Personal History

_____

_____

_____

_____

_____

_____

_____

_____

_____

_____

_____

_____

_____

_____

_____

_____

_____

_____

_____

_____

_____

_____

_____

_____

# My Organizations, Unions, and Clubs

## Personal History

I have belonged to the following organizations, unions, clubs, etc. (List all such organizations, with dates of membership, offices held, etc. If the organization is not commonly known, describe it.)

_____

_____

_____

_____

_____

_____

_____

_____

_____

_____

_____

_____

_____

_____

_____

_____

_____

_____

_____

_____

_____

_____

_____

# Miscellaneous

## Personal History

The following miscellaneous notes regarding my personal history may be of interest to my heirs:

_____

_____

_____

_____

_____

_____

_____

_____

_____

_____

_____

_____

_____

_____

_____

_____

_____

_____

_____

_____

_____

_____

_____

_____

# Miscellaneous *(continued)*

## Personal History

_____

_____

_____

_____

_____

_____

_____

_____

_____

_____

_____

_____

_____

_____

_____

_____

_____

_____

_____

_____

_____

_____

_____

_____

# CHAPTER 3

# Understanding My Insurance Policies

*I*nsurance offers a way to spread the risk of financial loss among many people. The payment of an annual premium protects the insured (to the limits of the policy) against losses from fire, theft, accident, liability, etc. Any loss is shared by all of those insured, saving the individual from financial disaster. The group, in other words, absorbs the individual's unexpected losses.

Life insurance is primarily intended to ease the financial loss to a beneficiary that results from the policyholder's death. Although death comes to everyone and cannot be considered "unexpected" in the long run, it can certainly be unexpected when it occurs. If something happens to you—death, an accident, a stroke, or other circumstance that prevents you from acting on your own behalf—your loved ones may have to file claims, cancel certain policies, or obtain new ones in order to protect your property. However, many policies go unclaimed because the policyholder's family or heirs were never told about them. For these reasons, it is important that your loved ones know about all of your insurance policies. Use the forms in this chapter to list your various policies with the names and addresses of the agents and companies.

The following is not a detailed breakdown of the many types of insurance available. It should, however, give you some information about the most widely used coverages to help you organize your own policies.

## LIFE INSURANCE

A life insurance policy pays a designated sum of money to the beneficiary upon the death of the insured. This money may be paid in a lump sum, in a monthly sum for the life of another, in monthly sums over a certain period, or in some other manner spelled out by the terms of the policy. Regardless of the method of payment, the sum is designated in the provisions of the policy. It may even pay double if your death is caused by accident—a so-called *double indemnity* policy.

A widely purchased form of life insurance is *whole life insurance.* This type of coverage provides a sum of money (face value) to be paid to the beneficiary at the time of the insured's death. The insured has paid the same annual premium since taking out the policy. The amount of the premium is determined by the age of the individual at the time the policy was purchased. The younger the purchaser, the smaller the premium on the policy. Variations in the method of payment for whole life insurance are available. For example, you might obtain a policy which requires annual premiums for 20 years. At the expiration of the 20-year period, the policy continues in effect for the balance of your life, but no more premiums are required. It is even possible to purchase a policy by making one large initial premium payment. Regardless of the method of payment, whole life insurance provides coverage for the rest of your life.

*Universal life* is a form of permanent life insurance in which the policyholder may vary the premium from year to year. The cash value reserve in the policy is credited with an interest sensitive rate on short-term investments and is adjusted periodically. A full disclosure is made to the policyholder each year, showing the interest credited, expense charges and the pure cost of the insurance protection.

*Variable whole life* and *variable universal life* are forms of permanent insurance in which the cash value reserves are invested in equity investments, such as stocks and bonds. The policyholder is able to select the investment from the menu offered by the insurance company.

*Term insurance,* on the other hand, provides insurance coverage only for a specified length of time. That is, you might purchase a policy that provides coverage for 5 years, 10 years, or 20 years. The annual premium for term insurance is substantially less than the annual premium for whole life insurance. For example, a typical annual premium for a one-year term policy might be $1 to $2 per $1,000 at age 25. The cost of purchasing the same coverage would gradually increase with the age of the purchaser. By age 55, that same coverage could run between $10 and $15 per $1,000, or about ten times the price given a 25-year-old. On the other hand, whole life insurance might start around $10 per $1,000 at age 25. The premiums would remain at that level throughout the life of the insured. To take out the same coverage at age 55, however, might run from $30 to $45 per $1,000, or three to four times the price given a 25-year-old.

Many term life insurance contracts provide that the policy may be renewed at the end of the term without providing further proof of insurability. The premium for the renewed term will be higher than for the original term. Other term policies provide that they may be converted, within a certain period, into a permanent type of life or endowment insurance without proof of insurability. Once again, the premium would be adjusted.

Regardless of the type of life insurance you hold, it is important that your insurance policies be readily available at death, that they be kept in a safe place, and that your heirs know their location. Some companies may require that your heirs surrender your life insurance policies in order to collect the proceeds. Contact the insurance company for instructions on how to file a claim.

Many employers provide life insurance for their employees, and partnerships often fund buy-sell agreements with life insurance. Be sure to include information about work-related insurance in the forms in this chapter.

## MEDICAL, HEALTH, DISABILITY, ACCIDENT, AND TRAVEL INSURANCE

Health insurance provides a means for paying hospital and medical expenses arising from sickness and accident. In addition, disability insurance policies are used to provide money for loss of income when an individual is unable to work because of sickness or accidental injury.

Many different types of accident and illness insurance policies exist. Some are so limited in scope that it seems necessary to be gored by a bull while riding a streetcar between midnight and 3:00 AM in order to collect on the policy. Other policies, however, provide very broad coverage, though each has its limitations.

*Travel policies* were the forerunners of the present-day health and accident policies. Travel policies may limit coverage to airplanes, automobiles, boats, and motorcycles, or they may cover an insured individual during a specified policy period, like the length of a vacation or business trip.

*Medical expense reimbursement policies* range from a policy that pays $10 for each day the insured is hospitalized to health insurance policies that cover almost every medical expense that the policyholder could incur. Because the coverages vary to such a great extent, the cost of health and accident coverage varies greatly.

A relatively new idea in health care insurance, health maintenance organizations (HMOs), now dominate the industry. These plans contract with specific doctors, hospitals, medical labs, and so on to provide services to its members for lower than usual costs. If you obtain your medical care from one of the medical providers that has a contract with the managed care organization, all you usually have to pay out of pocket is a nominal copayment. However, if you use a provider who is not a part of the HMO's network, you have to pay more out of pocket; in fact, you may have to pay the full amount of your medical care or treatment, depending on the HMO to which you belong.

You can also purchase *major medical coverage* to pay for expenses not covered by your basic health and accident policy.

## VEHICLE INSURANCE

Automobile insurance should be considered a necessity by the owner of any motor vehicle. In fact, many states require all drivers to be insured for liability to other persons for damages resulting from an automobile accident. Regardless of the law in your particular state, it makes good sense to insure yourself against the claims of others and against a loss that you might sustain as the result of collision, fire, or theft of your automobile. Similar coverages may be available for motorcycles, motorboats, snowmobiles, and other recreational vehicles you own.

*Liability coverage* protects you, to the extent of the coverage that you have purchased, against the claims of persons who claim to have been injured or damaged by your motor vehicle. The policy not only provides for payment of the claim, assuming it is valid, but also pays legal and other expenses for the defense of the claim.

*Collision coverage* pays for damage sustained by your automobile in a collision or upset. It is usually subject to a deductible amount that you must pay if you are at fault.

*Comprehensive coverage,* along with fire, theft, and windstorm coverage, protects you from damage (other than damage caused by accident) to your own automobile.

*Uninsured motorists' insurance* protects the persons in the insured vehicle when they are involved in an accident with an uninsured motorist. For all practical purposes, such insurance provides liability coverage for the uninsured motorist. The injured persons can look to their own insurance company to cover their losses—rather than to an uncollectible individual.

*Underinsured motorists' insurance* protects persons in an insured vehicle involved in an accident with a motorist who is underinsured. If, for example, the persons in the insured vehicle sustain $50,000 of personal injuries because of the negligence of a motorist who has only $20,000 of liability coverage, the underinsured motorists' insurance would pay the excess over $20,000 up to the coverage limits purchased by the insured.

*No-fault insurance* for motor vehicle accidents has been adopted by many states. Although provisions of the laws authorizing such insurance vary from state to state, the general idea of no-fault insurance is that automobile owners must provide their own insurance for any injuries to themselves or damage to their own property, regardless of who was to blame for an accident.

Except in certain circumstances, such as death, disfigurement, and impairment of bodily functions (as established by states' no-fault laws), an injured person cannot sue the other driver to recover any damages. In those states that have adopted the no-fault concept, the law requires that motorists maintain no-fault insurance on their vehicles. Generally, if you do not carry such insurance, you are not only violating the law, but you have no way to seek repayment of your losses in an accident, even if you are not at fault.

At the time of your death, the vehicle insurance company should be notified so there will be complete coverage during the period before the vehicle's assignment to its next owner.

## HOMEOWNERS AND OTHER RESIDENCE INSURANCE

Originally, fire insurance was about the only type of insurance that a homeowner could obtain on his or her residence. As the various insurance lines developed, insurance became available to protect against windstorm, hail, flood, explosion, riot, smoke damage, etc. Insurance also became available for the contents of the home, as well as for outbuildings.

Today, most homeowners purchase a homeowners policy that combines fire and extended coverage insurance on the dwelling with protection for personal property, additional living expense, and comprehensive personal liability coverage, including medical payments to guests and some direct damage to property of others. Rather than being required to purchase individual policies to cover each of these various risks, the homeowners policy combines them.

Similar types of policies are available to condominium owners and apartment dwellers. The policy can be tailor-made to fit specific needs by the addition of standard forms.

Upon your death, your heirs should immediately contact your insurance agent to ensure that your home and contents are properly insured during the administration of your estate.

## ADDITIONAL LIABILITY PROTECTION

Many insurance companies offer additional liability protection through an *umbrella policy,* which provides insurance coverage in excess of your regular automobile, personal liability, and other liability coverages. It is usually sold in multiples of $1 million and is a low-cost method of buying substantial protection.

# Life Insurance

*Types of insurance policies:* *WH = Whole Life* *UN = Universal Life* *TM = Term*
*DI = Double Indemnity* *VUL = Variable Universal Life* *VWL = Variable Whole Life* *O = Other*

(The above abbreviations may be used to describe the different types of insurance policies you carry.)

☐ I do not carry insurance policies.

☐ I carry the following insurance policies:

Company: _____ Type of policy: _____

Agent (if any): _____

Address and phone # of ☐ company or ☐ agent: _____

_____

_____

Policy #: _____ Face amount: _____

Beneficiary(ies): _____

❖❖❖❖❖❖

Company: _____ Type of policy: _____

Agent (if any): _____

Address and phone # of ☐ company or ☐ agent: _____

_____

_____

Policy #: _____ Face amount: _____

Beneficiary(ies): _____

❖❖❖❖❖❖

Company: _____ Type of policy: _____

Agent (if any): _____

Address and phone # of ☐ company or ☐ agent: _____

_____

_____

Policy #: _____ Face amount: _____

Beneficiary(ies): _____

# Life Insurance *(continued)*

*Types of insurance policies:   WH = Whole Life   UN = Universal Life   TM = Term*
*DI = Double Indemnity   VUL = Variable Universal Life   VWL = Variable Whole Life   O = Other*

(The above abbreviations may be used to describe the different types of insurance policies you carry.)

☐ I do not carry insurance policies.

☐ I carry the following insurance policies:

Company: _____ Type of policy: _____

Agent (if any): _____

Address and phone # of ☐ company or ☐ agent: _____

_____

_____

Policy #: _____ Face amount: _____

Beneficiary(ies): _____

❖❖❖❖❖❖

Company: _____ Type of policy: _____

Agent (if any): _____

Address and phone # of ☐ company or ☐ agent: _____

_____

_____

Policy #: _____ Face amount: _____

Beneficiary(ies): _____

❖❖❖❖❖❖

Company: _____ Type of policy: _____

Agent (if any): _____

Address and phone # of ☐ company or ☐ agent: _____

_____

_____

Policy #: _____ Face amount: _____

Beneficiary(ies): _____

# Life Insurance *(continued)*

*Types of insurance policies:    WH = Whole Life    UN = Universal Life    TM = Term*
*DI = Double Indemnity    VUL = Variable Universal Life    VWL = Variable Whole Life    O = Other*

(The above abbreviations may be used to describe the different types of insurance policies you carry.)

☐ I do not carry insurance policies.

☐ I carry the following insurance policies:

Company: _____ Type of policy: _____

Agent (if any): _____

Address and phone # of ☐ company or ☐ agent: _____

_____

_____

Policy #: _____ Face amount: _____

Beneficiary(ies): _____

❖❖❖❖❖❖

Company: _____ Type of policy: _____

Agent (if any): _____

Address and phone # of ☐ company or ☐ agent: _____

_____

_____

Policy #: _____ Face amount: _____

Beneficiary(ies): _____

❖❖❖❖❖❖

Company: _____ Type of policy: _____

Agent (if any): _____

Address and phone # of ☐ company or ☐ agent: _____

_____

_____

Policy #: _____ Face amount: _____

Beneficiary(ies): _____

# Homeowners or Other Residence Insurance

☐ I do not carry homeowners or residence insurance.

☐ I carry homeowners or residence insurance policies with the following companies (list all policies including fire, windstorm, theft, personal liability, homeowners, etc.):

Company: _____

Agent (if any): _____

Address and phone # of ☐ company or ☐ agent: _____

_____

_____

Policy #: _____

Description of coverage: _____

_____

❖❖❖❖❖❖

Company: _____

Agent (if any): _____

Address and phone # of ☐ company or ☐ agent: _____

_____

_____

Policy #: _____

Description of coverage: _____

_____

❖❖❖❖❖❖

Company: _____

Agent (if any): _____

Address and phone # of ☐ company or ☐ agent: _____

_____

_____

Policy #: _____

Description of coverage: _____

_____

# Medical, Health, Disability, Accident, and Travel Insurance

*Types of policies:*
*HO = Hospitalization*        *VI = Vision and Eye*        *MD = Medical*
*MM = Major Medical*        *SU = Surgical*        *ATR = Air Travel*
*DI  = Disability*        *TR = Travel Accidental Death*        *Accidental Death*
*DT = Dental*        *O  = Other*        *MC = Medicare*

(The above abbreviations may be used to describe the different types of insurance policies you carry.)

☐ I carry no medical insurance policies.

☐ I carry the following medical insurance policies:

Company: _____ Type of policy: _____

Agent (if any): _____

Address and phone # of ☐ company or ☐ agent: _____

_____

_____

Policy #: _____ Group #: _____ Service code #: _____

❖❖❖❖❖❖

Company: _____ Type of policy: _____

Agent (if any): _____

Address and phone # of ☐ company or ☐ agent: _____

_____

_____

Policy #: _____ Group #: _____ Service code #: _____

❖❖❖❖❖❖

Company: _____ Type of policy: _____

Agent (if any): _____

Address and phone # of ☐ company or ☐ agent: _____

_____

Policy #: _____ Group #: _____ Service code #: _____

# Medical, Health, Disability, Accident, and Travel Insurance

*(continued)*

*Types of policies:*
*HO* = *Hospitalization*    *VI* = *Vision and Eye*    *MD* = *Medical*
*MM* = *Major Medical*    *SU* = *Surgical*    *ATR* = *Air Travel*
*DI* = *Disability*    *TR* = *Travel Accidental Death*    *Accidental Death*
*DT* = *Dental*    *O* = *Other*    *MC* = *Medicare*

(The above abbreviations may be used to describe the different types of insurance policies you carry.)

☐ I carry no medical insurance policies.

☐ I carry the following medical insurance policies:

Company: _____ Type of policy: _____

Agent (if any): _____

Address and phone # of ☐ company or ☐ agent: _____

_____

_____

Policy #: _____ Group #: _____ Service code #: _____

❖❖❖❖❖❖

Company: _____ Type of policy: _____

Agent (if any): _____

Address and phone # of ☐ company or ☐ agent: _____

_____

_____

Policy #: _____ Group #: _____ Service code #: _____

❖❖❖❖❖❖

Company: _____ Type of policy: _____

Agent (if any): _____

Address and phone # of ☐ company or ☐ agent: _____

_____

_____

Policy #: _____ Group #: _____ Service code #: _____

# Vehicle Insurance

## Automobiles, Motorcycles, Boats, Airplanes, etc.

I carry vehicle insurance (including motorcycles, snowmobiles, boats, airplanes, etc.) with the following companies:

Company: _____

Agent (if any): _____

Address and phone # of ☐ company or ☐ agent: _____

_____

_____

Policy #: _____

Description of vehicles insured: _____

_____

❖❖❖❖❖❖

Company: _____

Agent (if any): _____

Address and phone # of ☐ company or ☐ agent: _____

_____

_____

Policy #: _____

Description of vehicles insured: _____

_____

❖❖❖❖❖❖

Company: _____

Agent (if any): _____

Address and phone # of ☐ company or ☐ agent: _____

_____

_____

Policy #: _____

Description of vehicles insured: _____

_____

# Vehicle Insurance *(continued)*

## Automobiles, Motorcycles, Boats, Airplanes, etc.

I carry vehicle insurance (including motorcycles, snowmobiles, boats, airplanes, etc.) with the following companies:

Company: _____

Agent (if any): _____

Address and phone # of ☐ company or ☐ agent: _____

_____

_____

Policy #: _____

Description of vehicles insured: _____

_____

❖❖❖❖❖❖

Company: _____

Agent (if any): _____

Address and phone # of ☐ company or ☐ agent: _____

_____

_____

Policy #: _____

Description of vehicles insured: _____

_____

❖❖❖❖❖❖

Company: _____

Agent (if any): _____

Address and phone # of ☐ company or ☐ agent: _____

_____

_____

Policy #: _____

Description of vehicles insured: _____

_____

# CHAPTER 4

# *Tapping into Other Benefits*

Most of us are aware of retirement benefits from Social Security, certain disability benefits for U.S. military veterans, worker's disability compensation for job-related injuries and illness, and retirement payments from private and public pension plans. But you may be unaware of the benefits from the same sources that may be available to your survivors. This chapter is primarily concerned with benefits that may be available to your survivors.

## SOCIAL SECURITY

Social Security provides continuing income when family earnings are reduced or stopped because of retirement, disability, or death. Nine of ten workers in the United States earn protection under Social Security.

Since Social Security legislation was enacted in 1935, many changes have broadened the protection given to workers and their families. Initially, Social Security covered only retired workers; but in 1939 the law was expanded to pay certain dependents of retired workers and certain survivors of deceased workers.

Disability Social Security insurance benefits were first provided in July 1957, giving workers protection against loss of earnings due to total disability.

The Social Security program was expanded again in 1965 with the enactment of Medicare, which provides hospital and medical insurance protection to people 65 and over. Since 1973, Medicare coverage has also been available to those people under 65 who have been entitled to Social Security disability checks for two or more consecutive years. It also covers people with permanent kidney failure who need dialysis or kidney transplants.

Before you or your family can receive monthly cash benefits, credit must be established for a certain amount of work under Social Security.

Just how much credit you must establish depends on your age and whether you are applying for retirement, survivor, or disability benefits. Information on specific requirements is available at any of the 1,300 Social Security Administration offices located throughout the country.

## WHO CAN QUALIFY FOR SOCIAL SECURITY BENEFITS

Retirement checks may be received as early as age 62 and disability checks at any age. Monthly payments can be received by a *retired* or a *disabled* worker's

- unmarried children under 18 (or 19 if a full-time elementary or secondary school student);
- unmarried children 18 or over who were severely disabled before age 22, and who continue to be disabled;
- a wife or husband 62 or older who has been married to the worker for at least one year; or
- a wife or husband under 62 if she or he is caring for a child under 16 (or disabled) who is receiving a benefit under the worker's earnings.

A divorced spouse who has been divorced at least two years can receive benefits at 62 regardless of whether his or her former spouse receives them. Their marriage must have lasted ten years or more; the former spouse must be at least 62 and eligible for Social Security benefits, regardless of whether he or she has retired; and the divorced spouse must not be eligible for an equal or higher benefit on his or her own—or anyone else's—Social Security record.

Your heirs are primarily affected, however, by benefits that may be available after your death—survivor's benefits. For example, your spouse and minor children may be entitled to a one-time $255 lump-sum payment.

Social Security survivors insurance can provide cash benefits on the earnings record of a deceased worker to the following:

- A widow or widower—full benefits (assuming the worker never elected reduced benefits for early retirement) at 65 or any age if caring for an entitled child (under 16 or disabled) of the deceased worker. Reduced benefits can be received at 60 (or 50 and disabled) if not caring for a child. Remarriage after 60 (or 50 if disabled) will not prevent the payment of benefits.
- Unmarried children up to 18 (or 19 if they are attending an elementary or secondary school full time). Children who were disabled before 22 can receive benefits at any age as long as they remain disabled.

- Divorced widow or widower if the marriage lasted at least ten years—full benefits (assuming the worker never elected reduced benefits for early retirement) at 65 or any age if caring for an entitled child (under 16 or disabled) of the deceased worker. Reduced benefits can be received at 60 (or 50 if disabled). Remarriage after 60 (or 50 if disabled) will not prevent the payment of benefits.
- A mother or father of the worker's child under 16 or disabled, if caring for the child.

In addition, grandchildren, great-grandchildren, and dependent parents 62 or older may qualify for survivors benefits on the deceased worker's record under certain circumstances.

*Medicare,* a federal hospital and medical insurance, is available through Social Security to help protect eligible persons 65 and over from the high costs of health care. Also eligible for Medicare are disabled people under 65 who have been entitled to Social Security disability benefits for 24 or more months. Insured workers and their dependents who need dialysis treatment or a kidney transplant because of permanent kidney failure also have Medicare protection at any age.

The *hospital insurance* portion of Medicare helps pay the cost of inpatient hospital care and certain kinds of follow-up care. If you are eligible for Social Security or Railroad Retirement payments, either as a worker, dependent, or survivor, you automatically have hospital insurance protection when you are 65. It is free to those who are eligible.

The *medical insurance* portion of Medicare helps defray costs of physician services, outpatient hospital services, and certain other medical expenses, as well as services not covered by the hospital insurance. This part of the Medicare program is optional—you can opt not to pay the monthly premium. However, the premium is quite small and is adjusted periodically to reflect the cost of care.

You should apply for your Medicare insurance at least three months before your 65th birthday in order for your protection to start at age 65.

## APPLYING FOR SOCIAL SECURITY BENEFITS

When you apply for Social Security benefits, you should have original documents or certified copies of the following with you:

- Your own Social Security card or a record of your number (if your claim is on another person's record, you will need that person's card or a record of the number)
- Proof of your age (a birth certificate or baptismal certificate made within five years after birth)
- Your marriage certificate if you are applying for widower's or widow's benefits

- Your children's birth certificates and Social Security numbers if you are applying for them
- The deceased worker's W-2 form(s) for the previous year or a copy of his or her last federal income tax return if self-employed (Without this information, those earnings will not be in the Social Security records and cannot be included when benefits are calculated.)
- Proof of divorce, if you are applying for benefits as a divorced spouse

The above information provides you and your heirs knowledge of certain rights that may be available to you or to them. *Because the Social Security Act can be amended at any time, this may not be the latest available information concerning benefits to which you or your heirs may be entitled. Contact the nearest Social Security Administration office for a full explanation of your rights under the law.*

## VETERANS BENEFITS

The Department of Veterans Affairs (VA) is charged with administering benefits available to persons who have served on active duty in the U.S. military service. The benefits depend upon the veteran's length of service, the era during which the service was performed, whether the veteran is disabled, whether the disability was caused by active service, and so many other criteria that it would take another book to set out the specific requirements.

Under certain circumstances, the following benefits (and many more) *may* be available to a veteran:

- Pensions for disability caused by service-connected injury or disease
- Pensions for certain nonservice-connected disabilities
- Automobile allowance for service-connected loss, or permanent loss of the use of one or both hands or feet
- Hospitalization benefits
- Alcohol and drug dependence treatment
- Nursing home care
- Outpatient medical treatment
- Prosthetic appliances
- Vocational rehabilitation and counseling
- Loan guaranty benefits
- Insurance
- Federal civil service preference

Certain benefits are available to your heirs if you were separated from the service under conditions other than dishonorable.

*Burial flag.* An American flag may be issued to drape the casket of an eligible veteran. After the funeral service, the flag may be given to the next of kin or close friend or associate of the deceased. Flags are issued at any VA office and most local post offices.

*Burial in national cemeteries.* Any deceased veteran of wartime or peacetime service whose last period of active service terminated other than dishonorably may be buried in a national cemetery. In addition, the spouse, surviving spouse, or minor children of an eligible veteran may be buried in a national cemetery. In each instance, space must be available. There is no charge for a grave nor for its opening and closing.

*Transportation of deceased veteran to a national cemetery.* The VA may pay the cost of transportation of a deceased veteran for burial in a national cemetery if the veteran died of a service-connected disability or the veteran was receiving disability compensation from the VA.

*Headstones or markers.* The VA will furnish, upon request, a headstone or marker to be placed at the unmarked grave of a veteran whose last discharge was other than dishonorable. This service is provided for eligible veterans whether they are buried in a national cemetery or elsewhere. A headstone or marker is automatically furnished if burial is in a national cemetery. Otherwise, application must be made to the VA. The VA will ship the headstone or marker, without charge, to the person or firm designated on the application.

*Reimbursement of burial expenses.* The VA is authorized to pay an allowance toward the funeral and burial expenses of an eligible veteran. A veteran not buried in a national cemetery will be paid an additional allowance for a plot for interment. If the veteran's death is service-connected or if the veteran died in a VA hospital, the VA is authorized to pay a larger sum for the burial and funeral expenses.

*Dependency and Indemnity Compensation (DIC).* DIC payments may be authorized for widows or widowers, unmarried children, and low-income parents of service personnel who die during active duty as well as veterans whose deaths were service-connected (when death occurred on or after January 1, 1957). The exact amount of the basic benefit is determined by the military pay grade of the deceased veteran. Payments are also made for children between age 18 and 23 attending school.

*Nonservice-connected death pension.* Surviving spouses and unmarried children under age 18 (or until age 23 if attending an approved course of study) may be eligible for a pension if their income does not exceed certain limits.

*Education for spouses, widows, widowers, sons, and daughters.* If a veteran is completely disabled or dies as a result of service, the VA will generally (but with some exceptions) pay to help educate the spouse, widow or widower, and each son and daughter beyond the secondary school level, including college, graduate school, technical and vocational schools, apprenticeships, and on-the-job training programs. Education loans are also available.

If you are a veteran, your heirs should seek assistance through the Department of Veterans Affairs in order to apply for available benefits.

For more comprehensive information about veterans benefits, request a copy of the *Federal Benefits Manual for Veterans and Dependents* from your local VA office.

## WORKERS' COMPENSATION

Workers' compensation laws have been adopted by all the states. Although their details vary greatly, the general purpose of workers' compensation programs is to provide income to workers who are unable to work as a result of an injury or occupational disease arising out of the worker's employment. While incapacitated, he or she receives a monetary benefit based on his or her average wage and number of dependents. In addition, medical expenses related to the injury are paid by the employer or the employer's insurance company.

Here, however, we are primarily interested in workers' compensation benefits available to dependents of a deceased employee. Ordinarily, the spouse and minor children of an employee who died as the result of a work-incurred accident or occupational disease are entitled to weekly payments for a certain period. Usually, the spouse is entitled to payments for a specified number of years or until remarriage, whichever is sooner; and the dependent children are entitled to benefits until they reach a certain age.

Ordinarily, the laws also provide that the widowed spouse, or the deceased employee's estate, is entitled to a specific funeral or death benefit.

It is important that your heirs be made aware of any life-threatening injuries or occupational diseases you incurred during the course of your employment. If your death is subsequently caused by such an injury or occupational disease, your dependents may be entitled to substantial monetary benefits.

In the forms provided at the end of this chapter, be sure to detail any of your medical problems that may be related to your employment.

## PENSIONS AND OTHER RETIREMENT PLANS

Many public and private employees are provided pensions through their jobs. Some pensions are entirely financed by the employer; others are cofinanced by the employer and the employee.

Currently, many employers offer 401(k) retirement plans that defer taxes on both employer and employee 401(k) plan contributions and earnings until funds are withdrawn from the plan, usually at retirement. (Tax penalties apply to early withdrawals, except in certain circumstances.)

Many persons, even if they are covered by a pension through their employment, have established individual retirement accounts (IRAs), often in addition to their 401(k) plans. The law allows a person who is under age 70½ and who has earned income to deposit up to $2,000, or the amount of one's earnings (whichever is smaller), into an IRA account each year. Spousal IRAs, generally set up on behalf of a nonworking spouse, are also available. Contributions to an IRA may be wholly or partially tax deductible, or nondeductible (depending on whether covered by a qualified pension plan, such as a 401(k), filing status, and modified adjusted gross income level). IRAs defer taxes on earnings from contributions until the funds are withdrawn, usually at retirement. (Again, tax penalties apply to early withdrawals, except in certain circumstances.)

Several other tax-deferred plans, accounts, etc., can also help an individual to defer taxes until, theoretically, he or she has reached an age where his or her earnings have begun to decline. For example, self-employed individuals may establish a Keogh plan which allows for larger, tax-deferred yearly contributions and greater benefits than does an IRA. Another tax-deferred retirement option for self-employed people is a simplified employee pension plan or SEP, which is a type of IRA.

Many more types of pension or retirement plans are available—"savings" plans, segregated asset account plans, annuity plans, etc. Regardless of what type of retirement plans you are participating in, it is critical that your heirs are aware of those plans. At your death, one or more of those plans may provide dependency payments to your spouse and/or minor children, or may provide a substantial pay-off to a designated beneficiary or to your estate. On the other hand, a plan may provide nothing at all.

In the forms provided at the end of this chapter, give your heirs information about any retirement assets in which you have an interest.

# Social Security Benefits

My name (from Social Security card): _____

Social Security #: _____    ☐ Male  or  ☐ Female

I ☐ have or ☐ have never filed an application for monthly Social Security benefits.

If so, the application was filed on ☐ my earning record  or  ☐ the earning record of:

_____
                 *Full name*                                     *Social Security number*

I received the following kind of monthly benefit: _____
                                                *(Retirement, disability, widow, etc.)*

I ☐ have worked or ☐ have not worked in the railroad industry at any time after January 1, 1937.*

My military service information is found on my veterans benefits form, page 101.

My marriage history and the facts related to my children are found in the forms located at the end of Chapter 2.

My Medicare information is found in the forms on pages 88–89.

My Social Security card is located: _____

Other documents pertaining to my Social Security status are located: _____

_____

*This may affect your Social Security.

# Veterans Benefits

☐ I have never served in the military service of the United States.

☐ I have served in the military service of the United States.

Full present name: _____
First                          Middle                          Last

Name served under: _____
First                          Middle                          Last

VA File #: C- _____    Social Security #: _____    Railroad Retirement #: _____

Date of birth: _____    Place of birth: _____

| Entered Active Service | | Service Number | Separated | | Grade or Rank and Branch |
|---|---|---|---|---|---|
| Date | Place | | Date | Place | |
| | | | | | |
| | | | | | |
| | | | | | |
| | | | | | |

My marriage history and the facts related to my children and my parents are found in the forms in Chapter 2.

I received the following military decorations: _____

_____

The following is a resume of my military career: _____

_____

_____

_____

_____

_____

_____

_____

*(may be continued on reverse)*

# Veterans Benefits *(continued)*

---
---
---
---
---
---
---
---
---
---
---
---
---
---
---
---
---
---
---
---
---
---
---

# Workers' Compensation

☐ I have never received workers' compensation benefits.

☐ I have received workers' compensation benefits.

Name of employer: _____

Address and phone # of employer: _____

_____

_____

Date of injury or occupational disease: _____

Name of insurance company: _____

Address and phone # of insurance company: _____

_____

_____

Insurance company's (or self-insured employer's) claim number: _____

Details of injury or occupational disease: _____

_____

_____

Duration of payments: _____

❖ ❖ ❖ ❖ ❖ ❖

In addition to the above, I have received the following serious injuries or occupational diseases during the course of my employment:

_____

_____

_____

# Pensions and Other Retirement Plans

☐ I do not have any pension rights.

☐ I have certain pension rights.

Name of payor: _____

Address and phone # of payor: _____

_____

Pension identification number: _____

There ☐ are or ☐ are not benefits under the plan to certain survivors upon my death.

❖❖❖❖❖❖

Name of payor: _____

Address and phone # of payor: _____

_____

Pension identification number: _____

There ☐ are or ☐ are not benefits under the plan to certain survivors upon my death.

❖❖❖❖❖❖

I ☐ have or ☐ do not have an individual retirement account (IRA).

Name of institution: _____

Address and phone # of institution: _____

_____

IRA account number: _____

❖❖❖❖❖❖

I ☐ have or ☐ do not have a Keogh pension plan.

Name of institution: _____

Address and phone # of institution: _____

_____

Keogh account number: _____

# Pensions and Other Retirement Plans (continued)

❖❖❖❖❖❖

I ☐ have or ☐ do not have a 401(k) plan.

Name of institution: _____

Address and phone # of institution: _____

_____

401(k) account number: _____

❖❖❖❖❖❖

Other retirement plan (describe): _____

Name of institution: _____

Address and phone # of institution: _____

_____

Account number: _____

# CHAPTER 5

# Shedding Light on My Banking and Savings Accounts

S ince post-Depression deposits have been federally insured against bank failure, Americans have been pulling their money back out of cookie jars and putting much of it into financial institutions such as banks and savings and loans. These businesses provide consumers places to deposit money for safekeeping, for check drafting convenience, and for earning interest on certain types of accounts. In return for these and other services, the businesses have the use of depositors' money for making loans and investments.

## COMMERCIAL BANKS

Commercial banks offer the widest range of services among financial institutions. They handle savings and checking accounts and make a wide range of short- and long-term loans for personal and business use. Many also provide estate and investment services.

*Savings accounts* are considered *demand deposits.* In other words, a depositor has the right to demand or to withdraw, any or all of his or her funds at any time during regular banking hours. Savings accounts bear interest, which is noted, along with deposits and withdrawals, in a passbook or savings account book, or simply on a periodic statement. A money market savings account pays a higher rate of interest than a standard savings account but requires that the depositor maintain a certain minimum balance in his or her account.

*Checking accounts* are another type of demand deposits. They allow the depositor to draw checks payable to anyone. Although checking accounts historically have not paid interest, and, in fact, have often had fees associated with them, many financial institutions now offer interest-bearing checking accounts, along with traditional fee-based checking plans.

*Certificates of deposit* and *money market certificates* are *time deposits.* Customers who use these financial instruments agree to leave their money in the bank for a certain period—for example, two years. During that time, they may not withdraw those funds without incurring significant interest penalties. In return for having this long-term use of the depositors' money, banks pay a higher rate of interest.

Any of the just-described accounts may be established in the name of a single depositor or may be owned jointly by several depositors with right of survivorship. With joint ownership, an account belongs to the survivors upon the death of a co-owner.

Factors that affect the interest you can earn on your deposit accounts include your bank's method of compounding interest and of crediting the funds you put in the account and the money you withdraw during a quarter. For many years it was usual for banks to compound interest on a quarterly basis. Now, many banks compound interest daily to maximize the return they offer their depositors.

As for how your bank credits the funds in your account, you should know whether it considers the first funds you deposit to be the first withdrawn (called FIFO—first in, first out), the last deposits to be the first withdrawn (LIFO), or if it calculates your interest on your low balance in a quarter. Without going into great detail, it is noteworthy that LIFO and a method called "day of deposit, day of withdrawal" (DD/DW) offer advantages to the depositor. Low balance and FIFO accounting methods may provide less interest on otherwise identical accounts, depending upon the activity in the account during the quarter.

Most banks insure their deposits through the Federal Deposit Insurance Corporation (FDIC). This governmental agency was established to protect people from losing their deposited assets if a bank fails. The amount of coverage is established by law. Be sure your bank provides this insurance and check the coverage limits. Incidentally, if the total amount of your deposits exceeds the maximum amount of deposit insurance your bank offers, to ensure that your funds are adequately covered, you can establish accounts in several name combinations (for example, husband alone, husband and wife, wife alone, husband and child, etc.) or, if necessary, in several banks.

## MUTUAL SAVINGS BANKS

Mutual savings banks are chartered in fewer than half of the states, mostly in the Northeast, and maintain about one-fifth of the nation's savings funds. These banks specialize in mortgage and home improvement loans and, until the federal regulations expire, are allowed by law to pay a somewhat higher interest rate on savings accounts than commercial banks.

## SAVINGS AND LOAN ASSOCIATIONS

A savings and loan association (S&L), or building and loan association, is a group of people who have pooled their funds in order to lend money. The money is primarily loaned for homebuying and building and for other construction purposes. The funds may be loaned to other members of the organization or to nonmembers.

Each investor in an S&L is issued a number of shares in the organization, according to the amount of money invested. The dividends earned by S&L shareholders are similar to the interest earned by bank depositors. Most savings and loan associations also have their shares insured by the Federal Deposit Insurance Corporation (FDIC).

S&Ls offer basically the same types of accounts as commercial banks.

## CREDIT UNIONS

A credit union is similar in nature and function to a savings and loan association. Credit union members, though, have some common bond for membership—they are employees of the same company, members of the same house of worship, labor union, farm group, etc. Members put their money into share accounts and receive shares of the credit union. The funds in turn are used to make short-term loans to credit union members.

Most credit unions honor the drafts of their members. Drafts are similar to bank checks.

## ATM AND DEBIT CARDS

ATM (automated teller machine) cards allow customers of financial institutions access to their accounts to make deposits and withdrawals and to transfer funds from one type of account to another. Many ATM cards also allow the user to make purchases in person using a PIN (personal identification number). The cost of purchases are subtracted, or debited, directly from the user's account (unlike a credit card that issues credit to the user for the amount of the purchase).

Similarly, many financial institutions issue debit cards that debit users' accounts for purchases but include broader purchasing powers, such as mail order purchasing. By using the computer networks and security procedures of major credit card companies, these cards rely on the card number, expiration date, and certain personal information to verify the identity of a mail order purchaser. Because the number on these debit cards can be used for purchases, it is important to notify the financial institution upon the death of the card owner to prevent unauthorized use.

## SAFE-DEPOSIT BOXES

Safe-deposit boxes provide a place for storing valuables at a small cost. Most banks rent safe-deposit boxes. A few safe-deposit companies provide this service as their only business.

The cost of renting a safe-deposit box is determined by its size. For a nominal fee, you can protect your stocks, bonds, wills, deeds, gold, silver, and other valuables from both burglary and fire by storing them in a safe-deposit box.

When you rent a safe-deposit box, you are given a key. When you want access to the items in the box, you must use both your key and a bank key simultaneously. Neither key alone will open the box. This is a safety precaution.

For further protection, you must also sign a slip each time you seek access to the box. Your signature will be compared to the signature you placed on file when you first rented the box.

A safe-deposit box, like a bank account, may be owned in a single name or jointly. Joint ownership gives someone else access to the box should sickness or absence prevent you from getting into it. In addition, joint ownership allows your co-owner access to the box after your death. Most states require a depository to seal a safe-deposit box upon learning of the death of a co-owner. However, it can be opened by a surviving co-owner in the presence of a state official, who will inventory the assets and deliver the inventory to the probate court. This process ensures that the assets of the deceased are properly reported to the court and that the applicable inheritance taxes are applied to the contents of the box.

Keep original documents that are valuable or irreplaceable in a safe-deposit box. Store copies of the originals in your personal home filing system. Also, be sure that someone knows where the key to the box is located. The forms in this chapter provide a place for you to provide that information.

# Accounts and Safe-Deposit Boxes

*Types of Accounts:*

     *S = Savings Account*     *C = Checking Account*     *CD = Certificate of Deposit*
     *MMC = Money Market Certificate*

(The above abbreviations may be used alone or in combination to describe different types of bank accounts.)

☐ I have no bank accounts or safe-deposit boxes.

☐ I have the following bank accounts or safe-deposit boxes:

Name of institution: _____

Address and phone #: _____

_____

Account #: _____ Type: _____ Owner(s): _____

Account #: _____ Type: _____ Owner(s): _____

Account #: _____ Type: _____ Owner(s): _____

Debit card #: _____

Safe-deposit box: _____ Key is located: _____

❖ ❖ ❖ ❖ ❖ ❖

Name of institution: _____

Address and phone #: _____

_____

Account #: _____ Type: _____ Owner(s): _____

Account #: _____ Type: _____ Owner(s): _____

Account #: _____ Type: _____ Owner(s): _____

Debit card #: _____

Safe-deposit box: _____ Key is located: _____

❖ ❖ ❖ ❖ ❖ ❖

Name of institution: _____

Address and phone #: _____

_____

Account #: _____ Type: _____ Owner(s): _____

Account #: _____ Type: _____ Owner(s): _____

Account #: _____ Type: _____ Owner(s): _____

Debit card #: _____

Safe-deposit box: _____ Key is located: _____

# Accounts and Safe-Deposit Boxes *(continued)*

*Types of Accounts:*

    *S = Savings Account*    *C = Checking Account*    *CD = Certificate of Deposit*
    *MMC = Money Market Certificate*

(The above abbreviations may be used alone or in combination to describe different types of bank accounts.)

☐ I have no bank accounts or safe-deposit boxes.

☐ I have the following bank accounts or safe-deposit boxes:

Name of institution: _____

Address and phone #: _____

_____

Account #: _____ Type: _____ Owner(s): _____

Account #: _____ Type: _____ Owner(s): _____

Account #: _____ Type: _____ Owner(s): _____

Debit card #: _____

Safe-deposit box: _____ Key is located: _____

❖❖❖❖❖❖❖

Name of institution: _____

Address and phone #: _____

_____

Account #: _____ Type: _____ Owner(s): _____

Account #: _____ Type: _____ Owner(s): _____

Account #: _____ Type: _____ Owner(s): _____

Debit card #: _____

Safe-deposit box: _____ Key is located: _____

❖❖❖❖❖❖❖

Name of institution: _____

Address and phone #: _____

_____

Account #: _____ Type: _____ Owner(s): _____

Account #: _____ Type: _____ Owner(s): _____

Account #: _____ Type: _____ Owner(s): _____

Debit card #: _____

Safe-deposit box: _____ Key is located: _____

# Safe-Deposit Box Inventories

Safe-deposit box # _____ inventory:        Safe-deposit box # _____ inventory:

_____        _____

_____        _____

_____        _____

_____        _____

_____        _____

_____        _____

_____        _____

_____        _____

_____        _____

_____        _____

_____        _____

_____        _____

_____        _____

_____        _____

_____        _____

_____        _____

_____        _____

_____        _____

_____        _____

_____        _____

# CHAPTER 6

# *Walking Through My Investment Portfolio*

The term *securities,* as used in this book, refers to investments, such as stocks, bonds, and mutual funds, commonly traded on stock exchanges or in the over-the-counter market. Such trades are usually handled through a stockbroker. Current exchange methods allow an investor to complete transactions almost instantaneously, making the purchase and sale of such securities a simple procedure, especially with the advent of online trading.

## STOCKS

A share of stock represents one unit of ownership in a corporation. Naturally, the percentage of ownership represented by one share of stock depends on the number of shares issued by the corporation. If only 100 shares of stock are issued, one share represents a 1 percent ownership interest in the corporation. If millions of shares are issued, one share of stock represents only a miniscule ownership interest.

*Common stock* is the basic corporate stock. If the corporation issues no other types of stock, common stock represents the entire corporate ownership. The common stockholders have the right to manage the affairs of the corporation through a board of directors, which they elect. If the corporation were to dissolve, its assets (after payment of its debts) would be distributed to the common stockholders in proportion to the number of shares they hold. Some companies may have more than one class of common stock, in which case one class usually has substantially greater voting powers than the other.

*Preferred stock,* as its name implies, has certain preferences over common stock. Many corporations do not have preferred stock. This type of stock might be established in the corporate charter when the corporation is formed, or later added to the charter by a majority action of the common stockholders.

The preferences, or priorities, given to preferred stockholders vary from corporation to corporation but are spelled out in each corporation's corporate charter. The most common preference is a priority in the distribution of profits. For example, preferred stockholders may be entitled to a fixed dividend before any dividends can be paid to common stockholders. Typically, they also enjoy the right to have any omitted dividends paid before a dividend may be paid on the common stock. Although these are often the only priorities given to preferred stockholders, they may also have a preference over common stockholders in the distribution of assets when a corporation dissolves. If that is the case, preferred stockholders are completely paid off before any distribution is made to the common stockholders.

To obtain these preferences, preferred stockholders give up certain rights. For example, they usually do not have the right to vote for the election of the corporate management team, nor the right to share in corporate profits for any more than their fixed preferential dividends.

Because the return on a share of preferred stock remains constant, the price fluctuations of preferred stock resemble the price changes of corporate bonds more closely than those of common stock.

## BONDS AND DEBENTURES

Most corporations need to borrow money from time to time due to cyclical money shortages, plans to expand facilities, or plans to develop new products, among many other reasons. They may borrow the money from a lending institution, or corporations may sell a series of bonds to investment bankers (called *underwriters*), who in turn sell the bonds to investors.

Corporations can issue a variety of types of bonds. The simplest form of a bond is called a *debenture.* It is a form of promissory note secured only by the corporation's financial ability to pay it when it becomes due. Along with preferred stocks, debentures are sometimes referred to as the "senior securities" of the corporation. Bondholders are entitled to interest payments before any dividends are paid on common stock, and they stand ahead of common stockholders in the distribution of capital if the corporation is dissolved.

When a corporation issues *mortgage bonds,* it uses certain designated assets of the corporation as security. If the company is unable to pay off the bonds when they become due, the bondholders have a priority claim against those assets. The corporation may also secure an issue of bonds by depositing certain collateral (usually stocks, bonds, etc.) with a trustee. A bond secured in this manner is called a *collateral trust bond.*

*Income bonds* promise to repay the principal on a designated date, but only if the corporation issuing them earns sufficient income.

*Municipal bonds* are issued by a state, county, city, bridge authority, or other political subdivision. Normally, they have the added advantage of being free from U.S. federal income tax liability.

We normally think of bonds with face amounts of $1,000. However, many bonds are issued for larger or smaller amounts. Interest rates on bonds vary greatly, from as low as 1½ percent or 2 percent to 15 percent or more. Because the interest rate on a bond is fixed at the time of its issue, its salable value will rise or fall depending on the actual rate of interest being offered in the financial community. For example, if the going interest rate is 9 percent, a $1,000 bond bearing 6 percent interest will not find a market and will have to sell for less than it would otherwise. On the other hand, if the bond bears an interest rate higher than the current rate in the financial community, it may sell for a premium.

The prices of municipal and corporate bonds appearing in your newspaper reflect a percent of the face values of those bonds. For example, if the face value of the bond is $1,000, a quotation of 95 means that the bond is being sold for $950. On the other hand, a quotation of 104 means the bond is being sold for $1,040. Quotations on government bonds are in decimals with the figures after the decimal point representing, curiously enough, 32nds of a dollar. A quote of 96.16 is equivalent to 96 16/32nds, or 96½, which would mean a bond with a face value of $1,000 would sell for $965.

## MUTUAL FUNDS

Mututal funds were developed, among other reasons, because some individuals did not have the confidence, the necessary "know-how," or the desire to learn to invest their money themselves. A mutual fund acquires a portfolio of securities through the mass purchasing power of many individuals. It is managed by professionals; so by selecting a mutual fund that purchases investments designed for your particular investment objectives, you get the benefits of professional management. (Note that unlike most checking and savings accounts and certificates of deposit, mutual fund investments are not federally insured, and, as risk investments, provide no guarantee of return of principal.)

Many types of mutual funds are available. Some funds invest in common stocks specifically for income, growth, or speculative purposes. Other funds limit their purchases to municipal, U.S. government, or corporate bonds. Still other mutual funds invest in companies within a specific industry sector—health care, the leisure industry, or financial services, for example.

Regardless of the type of mutual fund, you should know that certain funds are sold by stockbrokers, financial planners, or salespersons, and that you will be charged a fee or "load" when you purchase a mutual fund through one of them. Many funds even charge a load when you purchase directly from the fund management company, without benefit of investment consultation. A fund's sales charge will not necessarily indicate how well that fund will perform for you. On the other hand, "no-load" mutual funds are available through direct mailings, magazine and newspaper advertisements, discount brokerages, and some other financial institutions. Both load and no-load funds annually charge operating expenses or management fees to their shareholders. Some funds also charge 12b-1 fees for fund marketing expenses. Though loads, sales commissions, and fees affect the total return of a mutual fund, its performance generally has a greater effect on your return.

## MONEY MARKET FUNDS

A *money market fund* is similar to a mutual fund in that your investment is combined with other investments in order to create a large fund of money, which in turn is invested in commercial paper, certificates of deposit, and other short-term securities bearing high interest rates. Normally, earnings are determined daily and interest is continuously added to the investor's money market account. A money market fund does not offer a specific rate of interest (as contrasted to a bond), and its earnings fluctuate with the performance of the investments in the fund. The short maturity and diversity of investment in a money market fund is such that, normally, there is little fluctuation in earnings over a six-month period. In times of significant interest rate fluctuations, however, the return on a money market fund could also fluctuate considerably. Thus, an investor should continually check the performance of the fund so that he or she can withdraw the money if a change of investment appears to be advantageous.

Money market funds may be considered a parking place for money awaiting permanent investment. They provide relative safety of principal and a reasonable return of interest.

## COMMODITIES

The commodities market is based upon the paper sale, or purchase, of gold, pork bellies, corn, wheat, or other tangible goods for delivery on a specified date in the future. For example, if you agree to deliver a certain quantity of pork bellies in six months for $1,000, and in six months the price has dropped to $920 for that quantity, you can pick them up for $920 and deliver them at an $80 profit. If the price rises during those six months, though, you lose money.

Dealing in commodity futures is too highly speculative for the average investor. Although transactions require relatively small down payments, large profits or losses can occur. The losses could be many times the value of the small down payment. No matter how thoroughly familiar you are with the commodities market, regard any investments in commodities as very speculative.

## STOCKBROKERS

Stockbrokers are in the business of handling your securities investments. You can expect them to work with you to obtain your own investment objectives—current income, long-term growth, preservation of capital, or a combination of these. They act as your agent to buy or sell stocks and bonds and to provide records of purchases and sales. They give you the benefit of their knowledge of investments. For these services, you pay a fee based on the size of the transaction you make.

A reliable stockbroker is an invaluable ally who can help you acquire and manage your investment portfolio. Unless you have the time and ability to scrutinize the performance of the many corporations on the market, you will generally be much better off relying on the advice of a stockbroker regarding when and what to buy and sell. Large brokerage houses have staffs that analyze the performance and potential of various stocks.

When an account with a stockbroker is established, arrangements can be made for your stocks and bonds to be retained by the brokerage. If you do, the dividends and interest your investments earn for you are collected and sent to you as you wish and bonds that reach their maturity date are automatically presented for payment. A small fee is sometimes charged for this service, but the convenience, plus the monthly and quarterly statements, help you with your recordkeeping and tax preparation.

If you have the time and interest to keep abreast of the ever-changing securities marketplace, you may decide to direct your investment purchases and sales through a discount brokerage. While not providing advice on specific investment choices, discount brokerages often provide a wide range of general investment information to aid investors in their decision making, along with current price quotations, transactions via telephone or computer, and lower transaction fees than those charged by a full-service brokerage.

The forms in this chapter provide a convenient place for you to record information about the securities you own, where they are located and the name and address of your broker. Keep the listing of securities up-to-date. When you add or delete securities from the list, or even when you review the list, erase the date at the bottom of the page and insert the new date.

# Securities

## Stocks, Bonds, Debentures, and Mutual Funds

☐ I do not own any securities (stocks, bonds, debentures, mutual funds, etc.).

☐ I owned the securities listed on the next page as of the date the page was last revised.

☐ I have used the following brokerage firms for the purchase and sale of securities:

### Brokerage Firm #1

Name of firm: _____    Branch: _____

Title of account (e.g., trust, joint, etc.): _____

Address: _____    Telephone #: _____

_____

Account #: _____    Account executive: _____

### Brokerage Firm #2

Name of firm: _____    Branch: _____

Title of account (e.g., trust, joint, etc.): _____

Address: _____    Telephone #: _____

_____

Account #: _____    Account executive: _____

### Brokerage Firm #3

Name of firm: _____    Branch: _____

Type of account (e.g., trust, joint, etc.): _____

Address: _____    Telephone #: _____

_____

Account #: _____    Account executive: _____

*Circle "All of" or "Part of" where appropriate.*

☐ **All of / Part of** my securities are kept in my safe-deposit box.

☐ **All of / Part of** my securities are kept by   ☐ Brokerage #1   ☐ Brokerage #2   ☐ Brokerage #3

☐ **All of / Part of** my securities are located: _____

_____

# Securities *(continued)*

## Stocks, Bonds, Debentures, and Mutual Funds

C = *Common stock*   P = *Preferred stock*   CP = *Convertible preferred*   M = *Mutual fund*   B = *Bond*   CB = *Convertible bond*   D = *Debenture*
MMF = *Money market funds*

(The above abbreviations may be used to describe the different types of securities you have invested in.)

☐ I have not invested in any securities.   ☐ I have invested in the following securities:

| Company | CUSIP* (if known) | Type of Security | Number of Shares | Date of Purchase | Total Cost | Unit Cost | Adjustment to Unit Cost (Explain) |
|---|---|---|---|---|---|---|---|
|  |  |  |  |  |  |  |  |
|  |  |  |  |  |  |  |  |
|  |  |  |  |  |  |  |  |
|  |  |  |  |  |  |  |  |
|  |  |  |  |  |  |  |  |
|  |  |  |  |  |  |  |  |
|  |  |  |  |  |  |  |  |
|  |  |  |  |  |  |  |  |
|  |  |  |  |  |  |  |  |

*CUSIP (Corporation of Uniform Securities Identification Procedures) numbers are assigned to stocks and bonds to clearly identify the organization issuing the security.

The above list of securities was last reviewed, or revised, by me on: _____
Date

# Securities *(continued)*

## Stocks, Bonds, Debentures, and Mutual Funds

C = *Common stock*   P = *Preferred stock*   CP = *Convertible preferred*   M = *Mutual fund*   B = *Bond*   CB = *Convertible bond*   D = *Debenture*

MMF = *Money market funds*

(The above abbreviations may be used to describe the different types of securities you have invested in.)

☐ I have not invested in any securities.   ☐ I have invested in the following securities:

| Company | CUSIP* (if known) | Type of Security | Number of Shares | Date of Purchase | Total Cost | Unit Cost | Adjustment to Unit Cost (Explain) |
|---------|-------------------|------------------|------------------|------------------|------------|-----------|-----------------------------------|
| | | | | | | | |
| | | | | | | | |
| | | | | | | | |
| | | | | | | | |
| | | | | | | | |
| | | | | | | | |
| | | | | | | | |
| | | | | | | | |
| | | | | | | | |
| | | | | | | | |
| | | | | | | | |
| | | | | | | | |
| | | | | | | | |

*CUSIP (Corporation of Uniform Securities Identification Procedures) numbers are assigned to stocks and bonds to clearly identify the organization issuing the security.

The above list of securities was last reviewed, or revised, by me on: _____ *Date*

# Securities *(continued)*

## Stocks, Bonds, Debentures, and Mutual Funds

*C = Common stock   P = Preferred stock   CP = Convertible preferred   M = Mutual fund   B = Bond   CB = Convertible bond   D = Debenture*
*MMF = Money market funds*

(The above abbreviations may be used to describe the different types of securities you have invested in.)

☐ I have not invested in any securities.   ☐ I have invested in the following securities:

| Company | CUSIP* (if known) | Type of Security | Number of Shares | Date of Purchase | Total Cost | Unit Cost | Adjustment to Unit Cost (Explain) |
|---|---|---|---|---|---|---|---|
| | | | | | | | |
| | | | | | | | |
| | | | | | | | |
| | | | | | | | |
| | | | | | | | |
| | | | | | | | |
| | | | | | | | |
| | | | | | | | |
| | | | | | | | |
| | | | | | | | |
| | | | | | | | |
| | | | | | | | |

*CUSIP (Corporation of Uniform Securities Identification Procedures) numbers are assigned to stocks and bonds to clearly identify the organization issuing the security.

The above list of securities was last reviewed, or revised, by me on: _____
                                                                    *Date*

# CHAPTER 7

# *Locating My Real Estate*

*R*eal estate (or real property) is land and everything permanently attached to the land. A person buying real estate not only purchases soil, but the trees, shrubs, fences, and buildings that are on it. Your house is real estate.

## OWNERSHIP INTERESTS IN REAL ESTATE

The largest ownership interest available in land is called a *fee simple estate.* It provides the owner with complete control over the land—subject, of course, to zoning laws, chain of title restrictions, use of the land so that it does not interfere with adjoining property owners, etc. A fee simple estate is the type of ownership interest that is normally purchased and sold on the open market. Its name dates back to the early common law of England.

Although English common law provided for other types of estates, or interests, in land (fee simple conditional, fee tail, etc.), the only other commonly used ownership interest is the *life estate.* A life estate, created by deed or by will, gives a person the right to the use of certain property during that person's lifetime, or during the term of some other person's life. A son, for example, may deed his mother a life estate to a home. This would ensure that the mother has a place to live during her lifetime. However, upon her death, the full ownership of the property would revert to the son.

Real estate may be owned by one or by several individuals. If an individual is deeded a fee simple estate to the land, he or she has acquired the full ownership interest. That individual alone has the right to sell the real estate, transfer it by will, rent it, or use it in any other legal way.

When a fee simple estate is acquired by more than one individual, however, the deed establishes whether they are *joint owners* or *common owners.* Many sorts of property may be owned through these types of ownership—automobiles, stocks, bank accounts, real estate, etc.—and there are distinct differences between the two.

With both joint and common ownership, the owners have equal rights to use and enjoy the property during their lifetimes. Joint ownership, however, includes the *right of survivorship.* When a joint owner dies, the ownership of the property remains with the surviving owner(s). The last surviving joint owner ends up as the sole owner of the property. Another feature of joint ownership is that an owner cannot sell his or her interest unless the other joint owner (or owners) joins in the sale.

It is common for husband and wife to own real estate jointly as survivorship property. This avoids the necessity of probating the real estate when the first member of the marriage dies. However, survivorship property in real estate (as well as in bank accounts, etc.) could defeat the purpose of a tax-saving estate plan. Before entering into any survivorship property arrangement, discuss it with your estate planner.

A surviving parent sometimes attempts to avoid probate costs by establishing joint ownership of real estate with his or her children. This can create a number of problems (see Chapter 9) and is not normally recommended.

With common ownership, each person owns an undivided interest in the whole property, but there is no survivorship feature. Each of the owners may sell his or her undivided interest or may will it on his or her death to anyone. When friends join together to purchase resort property for general use by their families, they often take title as common owners. If one of the owners dies, that owner's estate, or heirs, would own his or her undivided interest in the real estate.

In nine states (Arizona, California, Idaho, Louisiana, Nevada, New Mexico, Texas, Washington, and Wisconsin), property acquired during marriage automatically becomes community property, so long as the spouses have no legal agreement to the contrary. Each spouse owns a 50 percent interest in all such property (except property received by gift or inheritance to one spouse, or unless it can be shown that the property was acquired exclusively through the means of one spouse from before the marriage). Married couples in community property states often prefer to hold title to property as community property because of possible tax advantages. Discuss this with your tax adviser or estate planner. Property held in the name of one spouse or in joint tenancy may be legally community property and may qualify for tax treatment as such, but the surviving spouse would need to prove that to the IRS. As with common ownership, each spouse has the right to assign by will the ownership of their portion of community property. If you live in a community property state, this will affect the property over which you have control in your will.

## SPECIAL USE VALUATION

Real estate is usually valued for federal estate tax purposes at its fair market value, based on its highest and best use. This could be a figure substantially higher than its fair market value for farming or business purposes—its use at the time of your death. And, of course, the higher the estate value, the higher the estate tax.

Your personal representative or executor may have the right to elect to value the real estate on the basis of the lower value. However, certain tests must be met. These tests are primarily concerned with ownership and land usage at the time of your death, to whom you leave the land, how long you have been using it for farming or business, etc.

If the above facts may apply to you, see your tax or estate adviser.

The forms in this chapter provide a place for you to list your ownership interests in real estate. You do not need to give the legal description of the real estate as it appears on the deed, but you should sufficiently identify the land so that it can be easily located. The deed by which you took title should be recorded at the county seat to give notice of your ownership interest in the land.

# Ownership Interests

## My Real Estate

CM = Commercial  F = Farm land  O = Other (describe)  V = Vacant land
CO = Condominium  I = Investment property  R = Residence

*(Use the above abbreviations alone or in combination to describe different types of real estate.)*

☐ I have no ownership interest in any real estate.

☐ I have an ownership interest in the following real estate:

Street address: _____

in the _____ of _____
    *Specify whether city or township*       *Name of city or township*

County of _____ State of _____

Type of real estate: _____

My ownership interest is ☐ sole, ☐ community property, ☐ joint with right of survivorship

with: _____

_____

or ☐ as a tenant in common with: _____

I acquired my ownership interest on or about: _____

My ownership interest became joint with right of survivorship on or about: _____

Purchase price of real estate: _____

I owe money on the real estate to:

 Name: _____

 Address: _____

   _____

On or about: _____ , I sold my ownership interest to:

 Name: _____

 Address: _____

   _____

for the sum of $ _____ , and I receive the sum of $ _____
per month from the sale price.

The deed, land contract, mortgage and records of property rentals, improvements, purchase, sale, etc., are located:

_____

# Ownership Interests *(continued)*

## My Real Estate

CM = Commercial          F = Farm land          O = Other (describe)          V = Vacant land
CO = Condominium          I = Investment property          R = Residence

*(Use the above abbreviations alone or in combination to describe different types of real estate.)*

Street address: _____

in the _____ of _____
          *Specify whether city or township*                      *Name of city or township*

County of _____ State of _____

Type of real estate: _____

My ownership interest is ☐ sole, ☐ community property, ☐ joint with right of survivorship

with: _____

_____

or ☐ as a tenant in common with: _____

I acquired my ownership interest on or about: _____

My ownership interest became joint with right of survivorship on or about: _____

Purchase price of real estate: _____

I owe money on the real estate to:

    Name:    _____

    Address: _____

              _____

On or about: _____ , I sold my ownership interest to:

    Name:    _____

    Address: _____

              _____

for the sum of $ _____ , and I receive the sum of $ _____
per month from the sale price.

The deed, land contract, mortgage and records of property rentals, improvements, purchase, sale, etc., are located:

_____

# Ownership Interests *(continued)*

## My Real Estate

CM = Commercial        F = Farm land        O = Other (describe)        V = Vacant land
CO = Condominium       I = Investment property       R = Residence

*(Use the above abbreviations alone or in combination to describe different types of real estate.)*

Street address: _____

in the _____ of _____
        *Specify whether city or township*             *Name of city or township*

County of _____ State of _____

Type of real estate: _____

My ownership interest is ☐ sole, ☐ community property, ☐ joint with right of survivorship

with: _____

_____

or ☐ as a tenant in common with: _____

I acquired my ownership interest on or about: _____

My ownership interest became joint with right of survivorship on or about: _____

Purchase price of real estate: _____

I owe money on the real estate to:

    Name:   _____

    Address: _____

            _____

On or about: _____ , I sold my ownership interest to:

    Name:   _____

    Address: _____

            _____

for the sum of $ _____ , and I receive the sum of $ _____
per month from the sale price.

The deed, land contract, mortgage and records of property rentals, improvements, purchase, sale, etc., are located:

_____

# CHAPTER 8

# *Uncovering Other Assets and Debts*

The preceding chapters provided forms for you to list your checking and savings accounts, life insurance, liability insurance, stocks, bonds, real estate, etc. This chapter is included to provide you with forms to list your miscellaneous assets and debts.

## ASSETS

Because forms cannot be tailor-made to cover the assets of everyone, this section provides a place to list a number of common assets—motor vehicles, airline frequent flyer miles (often transferable to your primary beneficiary unless otherwise assigned in your will), names and addresses of debtors—people who owe you money—business interests, whether you are beneficiary of a trust, whether you have an interest in a trust or real estate at the death of another person, and information regarding any claims or lawsuits you may have against other persons.

Additional space is provided for you to list any other assets of value you may own. Normally, it should not be necessary to list your household furnishings, because they are out in the open for your heirs to see. However, if some item of furniture has great value because of its antiquity, list it. The same applies to expensive paintings, coin or stamp collections, valuable jewelry, etc.

Have you loaned furniture to a friend or relative or to your office? Are any of the furnishings in your home borrowed from a friend? Have you already given an item to someone even though the item is still in your possession?

If there is any question as to whether a particular item should be listed, list it.

Each year millions of dollars in bank accounts, stock certificates, checks, bonds, dividends, and other assets are turned over to states by organizations that have been unable to locate the owners after the assets have been dormant for a period of three to seven years (depending on the type of asset and each state's laws). Although this book gives you a place to provide a complete list of your assets, if your heirs suspect that they have not located all of your assets, they should contact state unclaimed property offices, generally located in that state treasurer's office, in your state, and in any state where you might have owned real estate, had a bank account, or held other assets.

## DEBTS

Your heirs may have little knowledge of your debts. Naturally, you should not take time to list fluctuating monthly bills, such as utility bills. But if you have borrowed money from a relative, friend, or associate, tell your heirs about it. If someone has started a lawsuit against you, describe it and record the name of your lawyer.

# Assets—Personal Property

☐ I own the following motor vehicles:

| Year | Description | Balance Owed to: |
|---|---|---|
| | | |
| | | |
| | | |
| | | |

☐ The following persons owe me money:

| Name of Debtor | Address | Amount |
|---|---|---|
| | | |
| | | |
| | | |
| | | |

☐ I have frequent flyer miles on the following airlines:

| Airline | Frequent Flyer Number | Phone |
|---|---|---|
| | | |
| | | |
| | | |

☐ I have the following miscellaneous assets, which might be difficult for my heirs to locate or which might not be recognized as having significant value:

| Description | Location | Significance | Estimated Value |
|---|---|---|---|
| | | | |
| | | | |
| | | | |
| | | | |
| | | | |
| | | | |
| | | | |
| | | | |

*(Any of the above may be continued on page 138.)*

# Assets—Business Interests

☐ I have no ownership interest in any business.

☐ I have an interest in the following businesses:

Business name: _____    Type of business: _____

Address: _____    % of ownership: _____

Partner(s): _____    % of ownership: _____

_____    _____

_____    _____

❖❖❖❖❖❖❖

Business name: _____    Type of business: _____

Address: _____    % of ownership: _____

Partner(s): _____    % of ownership: _____

_____    _____

_____    _____

❖❖❖❖❖❖❖

Business name: _____    Type of business: _____

Address: _____    % of ownership: _____

Partner(s): _____    % of ownership: _____

_____    _____

_____    _____

❖❖❖❖❖❖❖

☐ I have an interest in the following patents and/or copyrights:

| Description | Pending? | Date Granted | Patent or Copyright Number | Termination Date |
|---|---|---|---|---|
|  |  |  |  |  |
|  |  |  |  |  |
|  |  |  |  |  |
|  |  |  |  |  |
|  |  |  |  |  |

*(Any of the above may be continued on page 138.)*

# Assets—Legal Action and Trusts

☐ I have a possible claim (personal injury, breach of contract, etc.) against:

Name: _____

Address: _____

_____

Description: _____

☐ I have a lawsuit pending against:

Name: _____

Address: _____

_____

☐ I have an uncollected legal judgment against:

Name: _____

Address: _____

_____

If you are not represented in the above by the lawyer listed in "Professional Advisers" on page 7, list your lawyer's name and address here:

Lawyer's name: _____

Address: _____

_____

❖ ❖ ❖ ❖ ❖ ❖

☐ I am the beneficiary of a trust.

Description: _____

Trustee: _____

☐ I am entitled to a remainder interest in a trust or in real estate at the death of:

_____

Description: _____

Trustee (if applicable): _____

*(Any of the above may be continued on page 138.)*

# Debts

☐ I owe the following debts, which have not been previously mentioned:
  *(Personal loans, car loans, other outstanding loans and notes, and NOT normal monthly bills)*

| To Whom | Address | For What | Amount |
|---|---|---|---|
|  |  |  |  |
|  |  |  |  |
|  |  |  |  |
|  |  |  |  |
|  |  |  |  |
|  |  |  |  |
|  |  |  |  |
|  |  |  |  |
|  |  |  |  |

❖❖❖❖❖❖

☐ I may be subject to a claim against me by: _____

Description: _____

☐ I have a pending lawsuit against me by: _____

Description: _____

☐ I have an unpaid legal judgment against me in favor of: _____

_____

Description: _____

☐ I have the following miscellaneous obligations or debts:

Description: _____

_____

_____

_____

*(Any of the following may be continued on page 138.)*

# Credit Cards

I have the following credit cards:

| Name of Company | Address/Telephone | Card Number |
|---|---|---|
|  |  |  |
|  |  |  |
|  |  |  |
|  |  |  |
|  |  |  |
|  |  |  |
|  |  |  |
|  |  |  |
|  |  |  |
|  |  |  |
|  |  |  |

# Miscellaneous Assets and Debts

# CHAPTER 9

# Declaring My Wishes— My Will, Trust Agreements, and Advance Directives

T he word *estate* brings to mind mansions, *objets d'art,* chauffeur-driven automobiles, and *money.* But do not be fooled. Anyone with a home, car, bank account, clothes, investments, or even the inherited gold watch from Granddad, has an estate. Your estate is the sum total of everything you own.

When a person dies, the assets in his or her estate are determined, funeral expenses and other debts are paid, inheritance and estate taxes are settled, and any monies owed to the deceased person are collected. After that, the remainder of the estate is distributed according to the directions expressed in the person's will. If there is no will, the assets are distributed according to the laws of the state in which the person lived. One who leaves a will is said to have died *testate* (leaving a *testament*—another word for will). A person who does not leave a will is said to have died *intestate* (without leaving a testament).

## PROBATE

*Probate* is the term used for the legal procedure established by each state, which leads to the estate's final distribution. The probate of an estate is supervised by a special court usually known as a probate court, or, in some states, a surrogate court or orphan's court.

Many believe that an estate does not have to be probated if the person who died, the *decedent,* has left a will. This is *not* true. Some legal authority must determine its validity, identify the heirs, pass judgment on claims against the estate, calculate the amount of death taxes to be paid, and distribute the remaining assets to the proper persons. Except for determining the validity of the will, the same procedure is followed for someone who dies intestate.

Filing fees, advertising expenses, appraiser's fees, etc., are minor costs in probating an estate. The major costs are attorney fees and fees for the personal representative charged with the management of the estate.

## EXECUTORS AND ADMINISTRATORS

If the decedent left a will, the estate's *personal representative* may be called an *executor,* since that person "executes" the provisions of the will. An intestate estate is "administered" by an *administrator.* The duties are identical; only the titles differ.

The personal representative is responsible for a number of tasks. He or she must collect the assets of the decedent; have them appraised; liquidate them to pay debts, make distribution to heirs, or pay the proper claims against the estate; prepare final income tax returns for the decedent; prepare state and federal inheritance and estate tax returns; distribute the remaining assets according to the terms of the will or the intestate laws of the state; record the necessary papers to clear title to real estate; and obtain receipts from the beneficiaries. After the receipts have been filed, the probate court discharges the personal representative.

The attorney for the estate guides the personal representative, prepares all legal petitions, orders, etc., and makes certain that the probate proceedings are proper.

In many states, compensation for the personal representative is set as a percentage of the inventory value of the estate. This fee is usually based upon a sliding scale. As the size of the estate increases, a smaller percentage is taken from the greater portions of the estate. For example, a personal representative might be entitled to a fee of 5 percent of the first $5,000 of an estate, 4 percent of the next $10,000, 3 percent of the next $35,000 and 2 percent of anything over $50,000.

Other states do not use a percentage figure but set the compensation in an amount that a probate judge has decided to be "just and reasonable." The amount of work involved by two personal representatives can differ considerably, even if each of the estates has a value of $100,000. Clearly it would be much simpler to administer an estate consisting of $100,000 cash, with no claims against it, than to administer an estate of $100,000 with real estate, stocks, bonds, and having many debts that must be investigated and paid. Completing the forms in this book could save fees in the probating of your estate.

## LOCAL ESTATE AND INHERITANCE TAXES

As part of the probate procedure, the estate's personal representative must pay all estate and inheritance taxes due to the state and federal governments. Almost all states in the United States have some type of death tax—either an inheritance tax or an estate tax. An inheritance tax is based upon the amount of *inheritance* received by each beneficiary. An estate tax is imposed on the total size of the *estate,* regardless of the size of the individual inheritances, adjusted annually for the cost of living from 1998 to 2006 according to the terms of the Taxpayer Relief Act of 1997.

Before calculating the amount of an inheritance tax or an estate tax, the laws usually provide that funeral expenses, valid debts, and lawful expenses of administering the estate may first be deducted. In addition, the tax rates and exemptions imposed on different beneficiaries may vary depending on their kinship to the decedent. For example, a spouse may have a total exemption on an inheritance. Parents, children, and grandchildren may have an exemption of $10,000. However, nieces, nephews, aunts, uncles, cousins, and nonrelatives may have no exemption. Then, for example, spouses, children, parents, and grandchildren may pay a rate of 2 percent on the first $50,000 inherited, 4 percent on the next $100,000, 6 percent on the next $300,000, etc. At the same time, all other persons may be taxed at 10 percent on the first $50,000, 12 percent on the next $100,000, and so forth. Usually, charitable gifts are not taxed so long as the recipient qualifies as a true, charitable organization.

With estate taxes, just like most income taxes, the lowest rate is applied to the bottom portion of an estate. As an estate rises in value, the tax rate increases, in stairstep percentages, on the higher values.

The taxable estate may not be the same as the inventory value of assets set by the probate court. For example, even though jointly owned property is neither probated nor generally subject to state death taxes, it is considered to be part of the taxable estate for federal estate tax purposes. Life insurance proceeds and almost any asset that passes to another individual at death are also subject to federal estate taxes, regardless of whether the state requires probate of those assets.

In a sizable estate, the federal estate tax can be very expensive. There are ways to minimize the taxes imposed upon your estate. *See a good estate planner.* If you do not know one, talk to your lawyer. If your attorney has the background to help you plan your estate, he or she will. If not, he or she can refer you to a qualified person.

## UNIFIED FEDERAL GIFT AND ESTATE TAX CREDIT

Estate planners often recommend giving gifts of the assets in your estate during your lifetime to reduce the amount of your estate subject to estate tax. A person who makes a gift (a donor) is subject to the federal gift tax. However, not all gifts are taxable. Each donor is entitled to a $10,000 annual exclusion on gifts to as many different recipients as he or she would like to give to. In other words, a donor can give $10,000 ($20,000 if a couple makes a gift) to as many different persons or organizations as desired without being subject to the gift tax. (Gifts of any size to a qualified charitable organization are not subject to this tax.) So long as you do not exceed your exclusions, you do not need to file a gift tax return. However, to have your gifts considered made one-half by you and one-half by your spouse, your spouse must sign the consent *on the gift tax return.* Be sure to state in your will that your gifts are not inheritance advances; in some states, probate courts may subtract the amount of your gift from the amount you provide that heir in your will.

You do not have to file a gift tax return to report gifts to your spouse regardless of the amount of these gifts; however, you must file a gift tax return if your spouse is not a U.S. citizen and the total gifts made to your spouse during the year exceeded $100,000. (A few other exceptions exist; see your tax adviser.)

You must file an annual gift tax return for gifts exceeding the exclusion amount. The amount of gift tax you will have to pay will be determined and applied against your lifetime unified tax credit. The amount of this credit is $202,500 in 1998, increased from $192,800 by the Taxpayer Relief Act of 1997. It is applicable to the combined total of gift tax and estate tax at your death and is equivalent to a combined taxable estate plus taxable gifts of $625,000. The 1997 act provides for annual increases in the amount of the unified tax credit until the year 2006, when it will max out at $345,800. That figure will be equivalent to a combined taxable estate plus taxable gifts of $1 million.

This chapter provides a form for you to keep a record of your taxable gifts for your personal representative.

## THE WILL

Your will allows you to make three important decisions that otherwise will be made by a judge in accordance with your state's laws. With a will, you

1. select a personal representative to settle your estate with the probate court and to make distribution of your assets.
2. appoint a guardian for your minor children if needed.
3. designate who will get your money and other valuables.

To prevent forgeries, fraud, and undue influence, each state has prescribed the method for a will to be executed. Although the requirements are relatively simple, they must be strictly followed or the will is not valid. States provide that the will must be identified as such by the signer to a certain number of witnesses. Then, usually, the signer and the witnesses must sign the will in the presence of each other. Unfortunately, many people attempt to save money by preparing their own wills but are not aware of the formal requirements of execution. As a result, their wills may not be legally valid.

It is not worth trying to save money by preparing your own will if you are not sure that you can write a valid will. See your attorney! Discuss how much he or she will charge and shop around, if necessary, for a fee with which you feel comfortable. An attorney should be able to prepare a simple will for a modest fee. An attorney not only knows the formal requirements for the execution of the will, but will be able to set out your desires clearly, minimizing the chance of some disgruntled individual contesting the validity of the will.

The laws of some states recognize that in some circumstances an individual may not have time to arrange for a proper will. For example, a soldier dying on the battlefield would have no opportunity to prepare and execute a will. In circumstances of impending death, some states will allow an oral (nuncupative) will. Don't rely on this! In addition, some states allow an unwitnessed will that is entirely in the handwriting of the testator (a holographic will). Don't rely on this either!

A will allows you to designate the beneficiaries of your estate. Generally, a man who leaves a valid will in effect at his death (a testator) cannot exclude his wife. If he does, the wife has a right to "take against the will" and receive a certain percentage (up to 100 percent) of the amount she would have received had there been no will. Some states have enacted similar provisions to protect the husband from exclusion by the wife's will. Except for the limitations involving a spouse, a testator can generally leave his or her estate to anyone.

## TRUST AGREEMENTS

A trust can be established in a will (called a **testamentary trust**) to accomplish many different goals. For example, a testator may have raised two of her children, at her expense, through a full college education. She may, however, have a young child at home. If her estate were left equally to the three children, the youngster would have to provide for his own upbringing and college education out of his one-third share of the estate. To avoid this injustice, the testator could leave her estate to a trustee (a bank, trust company, or trusted friend or relative, for example) for the use and benefit of all of her children. However, the trustee might be instructed that no division should be made of the estate assets until the estate had paid for the upbringing and college education of the young child. Many variations can be made of **when** inheritances should be paid, **how** they should be paid, and **under what circumstances** they should be paid. In effect, the trustee handles the estate for a certain period after the person's death in the manner the person has directed.

Trusts can also be used by an estate planner to help minimize the effects of estate taxation. Because this can become quite involved, discuss your particular situation with an estate planning specialist.

In addition to being established by a will, trusts can also be created during the person's lifetime. The individual enters into a trust agreement with himself or herself, or with a selected trustee, such as a bank. Trusts are generally established for estate planning or tax-saving purposes. Such a trust (created during lifetime) is called a **living** or **inter vivos** trust.

The individual can transfer ownership of desired assets to the trustee. At the individual's death, the trustee will distribute the remaining assets in the trust in accordance with the provisions of the trust agreement.

The *inter vivos* trust may be used to avoid the probating of a decedent's assets. Your estate planner can help you best determine whether this would fit your particular situation.

## INTESTATE SUCCESSION

If you die without a will (intestate), your estate will be distributed in accordance with the laws of *intestate succession.* The laws of your state of residence will govern the distribution of all your assets except real estate located in another state or country; the laws of the state in which the real estate is located determine the distribution of out-of-state property.

All states have established laws to determine the manner of estate distribution for an intestate decedent. Without these laws, there would be endless family disputes over the decedent's worldly goods. (If you don't think this is true, any lawyer will vouch for the family fights that take place even under the laws of intestate succession!)

It is always possible that your state's laws of intestate succession will provide the exact method by which you wish to divide your estate. But don't count on it. Because most persons want everything to go to their spouse, it seems strange that the various legislatures did not design it that way. In most instances, the surviving spouse receives 50 percent of the estate if there is one surviving child and 33⅓ percent of the estate if there are two or more surviving children. On the other hand, if there are no surviving children, the spouse normally gets 50 percent and the parents of the decedent get 50 percent. Check the laws of intestate succession in the state in which you reside and in any other state in which you own real estate. If something like this is what you want, you may be able to sit back and do nothing, though this is risky. On the other hand, if you want your assets specifically distributed according to your wishes, have your attorney prepare a will that reflects those wishes.

## JOINTLY OWNED PROPERTY

The intestate succession laws or directions of your will affect only property that *you* own at the time of your death. Many people own real estate, bank accounts, automobiles, etc., in joint names, with right of survivorship, with their spouse or with someone else. At the death of a co-owner, joint property automatically belongs to the surviving co-owner. In other words, *joint property is not an asset of the decedent's estate.* Neither the will nor the laws of intestate succession can control the distribution of joint property. You must take this into consideration for your after-death planning.

Joint ownership offers certain advantages in estate planning. However, if you rely solely on joint ownership to effect a plan of estate distribution, you may end up defeating the equitable distribution you had envisioned.

For example, suppose that your spouse dies before you and that you have three adult children who, in turn, have children. To avoid the expense of probate (because jointly owned property does not require probate administration), it might seem logical to place your home in the names of yourself and each of your three children, jointly. Then, upon your death, the three children would be joint co-owners of the home. It's that simple, right? Not necessarily. Too many things can happen. Suppose child A dies shortly after your death. Now the home is owned by children B and C—to the exclusion of child A's children. Or suppose you subsequently decide that you wish to sell the home, and one of your children, for whatever reason, refuses to approve the sale. An expensive legal proceeding could force the sale, but the unwilling child might be entitled to one-fourth of the proceeds. Or suppose one of the children becomes mentally incompetent and cannot join in a sale of the real estate. Then, although a guardian could be appointed to enter into the sale, the incompetent child's estate would have to receive one-fourth of the proceeds. Or suppose you and your three children are killed in an automobile accident, but that child C dies five minutes later than the other three co-owners. Under those circumstances, child C's estate would be the sole owner of the real estate because that child had outlived the other joint co-owners.

Joint ownership of real estate, bank accounts, etc., may have a definite place in your estate planning; however, be sure you know what you are doing and talk it over with your lawyer. *Remember, your will does not control jointly owned property.*

## YOUR WILL AND LIFE INSURANCE

The beneficiaries of your life insurance are determined by the life insurance contract between you and the insurance company. Neither your will nor the laws of intestate succession can designate to whom life insurance proceeds shall be paid. Of course, if your insurance contract designates your estate as the beneficiary of the insurance policy, the insurance company will pay the proceeds to your personal representative, who, in turn, will distribute the proceeds to the estate beneficiaries.

As you can see, the execution of a will does not cover everything. But with careful planning and professional advice, you can maximize the likelihood of having your wishes carried out exactly as you expect.

## POWER OF ATTORNEY

Using a legal document called a *power of attorney,* you can authorize a trusted friend, relative, or professional adviser to act during your lifetime on your behalf in legal, business, financial, health care, and other matters. Although the person you appoint is called your *attorney-in-fact*, he or she does not need to be a lawyer. (Do not confuse an attorney-in-fact with your personal representative, or executor. Your attorney-in-fact acts on your behalf while you are alive; your personal representative, executor, or administrator handles your financial affairs after you die.)

You can create a power of attorney with very broad or very specific decision-making powers, for a limited or indefinite period, effective immediately, or at some time in the future. For example, you can create a power of attorney that limits your attorney-in-fact to negotiating the sale of your car and signing papers associated with that sale. Investors often sign a limited power of attorney to allow their financial advisers to buy and sell investments for them. You can also create a more comprehensive power of attorney for financial management that allows your attorney-in-fact to handle all of your business and financial affairs—paying bills; buying and selling stocks, real estate, and other assets; making and carrying out business decisions; signing legal contracts; and so forth.

You can change your power of attorney at any time, as long as you remain competent. Unless your power of attorney document states otherwise, it normally remains in effect only as long as you remain competent. If you become incapacitated, your power of attorney becomes void. A *durable power of attorney*, however, remains in effect even if you become incompetent. You can also create a "springing" durable power of attorney that "springs" into effect only if you become legally incompetent. (See an explanation of durable power of attorney for health care in the following discussion of advance directives.)

Power of attorney documents are signed, witnessed, and notarized. Normally a lawyer draws up such documents to ensure their validity, but blank power of attorney forms are also available at many office supply stores. If you prepare your own power of attorney using a store-bought form, it's advisable to have an attorney look it over so you can be sure it will do what you want it to do.

It is a good idea to create two separate durable powers of attorney: one for health care and one for financial management. This enables you to select persons you trust to manage your financial affairs and make vital health care decisions should you become incapacitated. Frequently, the person you would trust to make financial decisions for you is not someone you would want dealing with your health care and vice versa.

## ADVANCE DIRECTIVES

Some individuals would prefer to die with the dignity of accepting their natural mortality rather than being kept "alive" through aggressive medical treatment and technology that only delays death when there is little serious hope for recovery. If this is your wish as well, you should provide instructions regarding your future medical care through one, or both, types of signed, legal documents called *advance directives.*

One type of advance directive is a *living will.* In this legal document, you inform your heirs, your physicians, and other concerned individuals, of your desires regarding your medical treatment and care in the event you become unable to speak for yourself.

The other advance directive is a ***durable power of attorney for health care.*** With this option, you appoint someone you trust to act as your health care agent, or proxy, to make medical decisions on your behalf if you are not physically or mentally capable of making them yourself. The person to whom you give a durable power of attorney for health care will have the legal power and flexibility to respond to special circumstances and to support your wishes if your health care providers or your family members resist following them.

All 50 states and the District of Columbia now have laws recognizing some form of advance directive. In declaring your wishes, these legal documents spare your survivors from making such decisions without knowing your preferences.

Three myths often keep people from executing advance directives:

*Myth #1:* Once you sign an advance directive, you give up control over your own health care. In fact, an advance directive takes effect only if two conditions exist: You are dying and you are no longer able to speak for yourself.

*Myth #2:* Once you sign an advance directive, you cannot easily change your wishes. In fact, you can simply tear up an old advance directive and draw up a new one.

*Myth #3:* An advance directive is a complex legal document, and preparing one is expensive because you need to hire an attorney. In fact, you can order an advance directive packet, specific to your state, by contacting Choice in Dying, a national nonprofit organization (Box 397, Newark, NJ 07101-9792; 800-989-WILL). The packet costs $5 and includes a guide for filling out the advance directive forms provided. Choice in Dying also will answer your questions on preparing advance directives and provide free consultation to your family members if you are dying.

Whether you choose one type of advance directive or both (for added clarity), discuss your wishes with your family, your personal doctor, and others concerned, and give them copies of your advance directives. If you appoint a health care agent, it is especially important to discuss thoroughly with him or her the sort of care you would and would not want. (In studies of family members who had not had these discussions, nearly a third of the families guessed the wrong type of treatment a patient would choose.) Review your advance directive each year to ensure that it continues to reflect your wishes and keep it in a handy place (not in a safe-deposit box), where your heirs can get to it quickly.

# My Will

## General Instructions

☐ I do not have a last will and testament.

☐ I executed my last will and testament on: _____

Attorney's name and law firm: _____

Address and phone #: _____

_____

Personal representative's name: _____

Address and phone #: _____

_____

My will ☐ does ☐ does not include a testamentary trust.

Trustee's name: _____

Address and phone #: _____

_____

Witness's name: _____
                        *Further identification (neighbor, coworker, etc.)*

Address and phone #: _____

_____

Witness's name: _____
                        *Further identification (neighbor, coworker, etc.)*

Address and phone #: _____

_____

Witness's name: _____
                        *Further identification (neighbor, coworker, etc.)*

Address and phone #: _____

_____

# Codicils, Trusts, Durable Power of Attorney for Financial Management

I have executed _____ codicils to the will on the following dates: _____

New personal representative's name (if changed): _____

Address and phone #: _____

_____

New trustee's name (if changed): _____

Address and phone #: _____

_____

Witness's name: _____

Address and phone #: _____

_____

Witness's name: _____

Address and phone #: _____

_____

❖❖❖❖❖❖

☐ I have not executed a living trust agreement that is in effect at this time.

☐ I entered into a living trust agreement on _____ with:

Trustee's name: _____

Address and phone #: _____

_____

Trustee's name: _____

Address and phone #: _____

_____

❖❖❖❖❖❖

I ☐ have ☐ do not have a durable power of attorney for financial management.

Attorney-in-fact's name: _____

Address and phone #: _____

_____

# My Advance Directives

## Living Will or Durable Power of Attorney for Health Care

☐ I do not have a living will or durable power of attorney for health care.

☐ I have expressed in a living will my wishes regarding my medical care if I become unable physically or mentally to make my own health care decisions. My living will is located:

_____

My most current living will is dated _____.

☐ I have executed a durable power of attorney for health care (or health care proxy) delegating the following person as my health care agent:

Name: _____

Address and phone #: _____

_____

My durable power of attorney for health care (or health care proxy) is located: _____

_____

My most current durable power of attorney for health care (or health care proxy) is dated

_____.

☐ (Optional) My advance directive is registered with Choice in Dying (Box 397, Newark, NJ 07101-9792; 800-989-WILL).

# Gifts

☐ I have made no gifts in excess of $10,000.

☐ I have made the following gifts in excess of $10,000:

| To Whom (Donee) | Date | Gift | Value |
|---|---|---|---|
|  |  |  |  |
|  |  |  |  |
|  |  |  |  |
|  |  |  |  |
|  |  |  |  |
|  |  |  |  |
|  |  |  |  |
|  |  |  |  |
|  |  |  |  |
|  |  |  |  |

I have filed the following federal gift tax returns:

| Period Covered | Internal Revenue Office Where Filed |
|---|---|
|  |  |
|  |  |
|  |  |
|  |  |
|  |  |

# CHAPTER 10

# Fulfilling My Final Wishes

O ne of the kindest things you can do for your heirs is to spare them the distress of facing decisions about your final arrangements. You can do this by making those decisions yourself and sharing them in this book.

This chapter does not suggest that one choice is better than another; it simply explains available options. The choice is entirely yours. You may prefer simple or elaborate arrangements; a funeral or memorial service; burial, entombment, or cremation; or bequeathal of your body to a medical school. Whatever you choose, *tell it to your heirs!*

Your first decision is whether you wish to share the gift of your organs and/or tissues with someone needing a transplant. If so, sign and carry the uniform donor card located in this chapter. Then you need to consider how you would like your remains handled. Your choice may be influenced by your personal wishes, your religious background, comparative costs and other factors. For example, not all religions accept cremation.

Next, depending on how you have chosen to handle your remains, you will need to consider whether you prefer a funeral (body present), memorial service (body not present), or no formal gathering. If you choose to have a funeral, you must decide whether it is to be public or private; whether you want an open or closed casket; who is to be the funeral director; whether you want flowers; whether you have any music preference; whether you want a eulogy and who will make it; whether you want a religious leader to preside; whether there should be a graveside service for the commitment of your body; whether you wish memorial donations to be made to a specific organization; and whether you wish the service to be held in a church or a funeral home. There are a lot of decisions, aren't there? To make certain your preferences are known, it is best to photocopy the completed forms in this chapter and give them to your next of kin and to the funeral director or memorial society of your choice. If you wish, you can even write your own obituary since you know your personal history best.

## UNIFORM DONOR CARD

The federal Uniform Anatomical Gift Act, which has been adopted by all 50 states, provides a process for an individual to donate his or her body for anatomical study, or to donate his or her organs and tissues for transplant. The process involves executing a prescribed legal document signed by the donor and two witnesses. This document has been reduced to wallet-size in the uniform donor card so it can be carried by the donor. Because speed is essential for organ transplants, the donor should carry the uniform donor card at all times so that it is readily available if he or she dies as the result of an accident or sudden injury. If you are interested in learning more about this subject, write to the U.S. Department of Health and Human Services, Washington, D.C., and request Publication No. (NIH) 79–776. Many states print a uniform donor card on the backs of drivers' licenses. The front and back of two uniform donor cards appear in the forms on pages 161 and 162. You can remove and carry them in your wallet.

If you are carrying a uniform donor card at the time of your death, your wishes may not be followed by the doctors who are caring for you if your next of kin is opposed to the donation. Therefore, make sure that your next of kin knows your wishes and is willing to abide by them.

## GIVING THE GIFT OF LIFE—ORGAN AND TISSUE DONATION

You may want to donate certain organs and/or tissues for use as transplants. These donations have saved and enhanced thousands of lives. Yet each day eight patients die for lack of available organs and tissues. Kidneys are in greatest need. Your donated organ or tissue may save one of these lives. Be aware however, that some medical schools will not accept your body for anatomical study if you have made an organ or tissue donation (with the exception of cornea donations).

If you want your organs or tissues to be donated, there is no cost to your family or your estate. Expenses associated with the donation are paid by the recipient. For organs (kidneys, heart, lungs, pancreas, and liver) to be viable, they must be removed prior to death from persons on life support systems who have no brain activity and are therefore considered legally brain dead. Tissues, defined for donation purposes as all other transplantable parts, such as corneas, skin, bone, inner ear, heart valves, and blood vessels, can be removed shortly after death.

After the organs and/or tissues have been removed, the remains of the deceased can be buried, entombed, or cremated exactly as though the body were intact.

## BEQUEATHING YOUR BODY TO A MEDICAL SCHOOL

You may wish to donate your body for medical education. The Uniform Anatomical Gift Act allows you to give your body to medical schools or hospitals for scientific use. Many feel that this is the least costly way of handling your remains. For that reason, many medical schools have an ample supply of bodies and will only accept body bequeathals from those who have made prearrangements with the school. However, some schools desperately need donations.

Because rules and regulations differ among the various medical schools, familiarize yourself with the requirements of the particular medical school you have selected. For example, some schools require embalming; others forbid it. Some pay all costs of transporting a body; some pay none. Individual schools are glad to provide you with printed materials describing their requirements and telling you how to donate your body. If you would like to investigate this option but do not know where to start, you can contact the National Anatomical Service (800-727-0700) for the name of the medical school nearest you and for the person at the school to contact for more information.

The medical school can arrange for the disposition of your remains following the useful educational life of your body. This will be done at no cost to your family. If your family wishes to have your cremated remains, arrangements may be made with the medical school.

## CREMATION

*Cremation* is a method of disposing of a body by placing it in a special furnace that reduces it to ashes. Although fewer than 10 percent of the bodies in the United States are cremated, cremation is used widely in certain parts of the world. In fact, the word *funeral* is derived from an old word of northern India that means "smoke." Today, many people of India burn their dead on funeral pyres and scatter the ashes on the sacred river Ganges. The Vikings placed their dead in boats, set the boats afire, and sent them out to sea.

Following cremation, the ashes are returned to the heirs in a box or urn and may be scattered, buried, or placed in a niche or vault in a *columbarium.* A columbarium is a building constructed for this particular purpose.

If you are basing your decision about what to do with your body solely on cost, cremation is clearly less expensive than burial or entombment because you do not need to buy a cemetery lot or mausoleum crypt, a grave marker, or monument. However, many crematoriums require that the body be placed in a casket at the time of cremation, so an inexpensive casket may be needed.

## BURIAL AND ENTOMBMENT

*Burial in the earth* is, by far, the most common method in the United States of dealing with the remains. Although early Americans usually buried a body in a family or churchyard cemetery, all the states now have regulations requiring burial in licensed cemeteries. The body is placed in a casket, lowered into the ground, and covered with earth.

*Caskets,* or *coffins,* encase the corpse for burial purposes. They can vary from a simple pine box to an elaborate bronze coffin with an inner-spring mattress. The cost of the casket greatly affects the total charges for the funeral.

*Vaults* of concrete, or similar materials, are often used to surround the casket to help prevent water seepage and to prevent settling of the soil as a wooden coffin disintegrates.

*Cemetery lots* for earth burial may be purchased for individual caskets. Larger lots may be purchased for future use by an entire family. Most cemeteries now include in the sale price of the lot a charge for its perpetual care.

The *cost of cemetery lots* varies enormously. In urban areas costs are generally more than in rural areas because property values are higher. However, even in the same community, costs can vary widely from one cemetery to another; and indeed, substantial price differences can exist in the same cemetery. A gravesite located on a hill, for example, may be much more expensive than a cemetery lot on lower ground.

*Entombment* is similar to burial in the earth, except that the casket is placed in a private tomb or in a *crypt* located in a building called a *mausoleum.* Mausoleums can be one or many stories in height. Crypts can be purchased for individual caskets or for a family of caskets.

If you choose to be buried in a cemetery or entombed in a mausoleum, tell your heirs where this should take place. In other words, *select your cemetery or mausoleum.* You do not need to purchase a cemetery lot or crypt. Such a purchase is recommended, though, if you are certain that you do not intend to move from the area, or if you wish to use a specific cemetery or mausoleum regardless of future moves. Many people plan to retire to warmer climates or other desirable spots, if they can afford this luxury. If you have made a firm decision about this, purchase your lot or crypt. On the other hand, if you are not sure about your ultimate living site, merely note your preference of cemetery or mausoleum. Make sure that the cemetery of your choice allows burial without a vault, if you prefer this type of burial.

*Monuments, headstones, and grave markers* may be used in cemeteries to identify the person buried. Monuments and headstones are generally made of stone and extend above the ground in varying heights. Grave markers are generally made of metal or stone and are placed flat on the ground. Many of the newer cemeteries require flat grave markers so that large mowing machines can operate freely. Where there are monuments or headstones, lawns must be mowed by hand—meaning higher labor costs. If you prefer a monument atop your grave, make sure that the cemetery you choose will allow it.

While you are making these decisions, you might as well determine the wording on your monument or marker. Although the majority of grave markers and monuments merely give the name of the grave occupant, the year of birth and the year of death, many monuments have epitaphs chosen by the deceased or his or her heirs. Note any specific directions you might have for this.

If you are a U.S. veteran and if your last discharge was other than dishonorable, the Department of Veterans Affairs (VA) will furnish, upon request, a headstone or marker for your unmarked grave. In addition, you, your spouse, or minor children may be buried in any National Cemetery in which space is available. (See Chapter 4.)

## FUNERAL SERVICES

*Funeral services* consist of the observances held for a deceased person before a burial or cremation. These services may include religious rites, a wake, fraternal or military procedures, a commitment service at graveside, and so forth. In this book, the term *funeral services* refers to ceremonies conducted with the body of the deceased present. If the body is not present, the last observances are called *memorial services.*

A *funeral director* is a person who, as the name implies, makes all the funeral arrangements according to the desires of the family, notifies the newspapers, makes specific arrangements with the deceased's religious leader, makes arrangements with the cemetery or crematorium, and prepares the body for burial or cremation. The funeral director generally stocks an array of caskets in various price ranges so that the family may select the best one for its needs. In addition, the funeral director is generally familiar with the requirements of life insurance companies, unions, Social Security, and the Department of Veterans Affairs, and can help the family of the deceased file the papers necessary to obtain any benefits they might be entitled to. Obviously, this individual can be invaluable to a bereaved family.

Your family may be emotionally distraught following your death and may, out of feelings of guilt or loss, spend much more money for the funeral than you would want. Therefore, it is important that you provide your family with guidance as to your wishes.

You can express your wishes on the cost of the funeral by filling out the appropriate forms in this chapter, or you can prearrange your own funeral with the funeral director right now. Not only can you make the specific arrangements, you can also arrange for prepayment. Because of a history of abuses by a few members of the funeral industry, most states have established rules and conditions to protect funeral investors from fraud. For example, in many states the money for prepaid funeral arrangements is deposited in a bank account in the joint names of the arranger and the funeral director, and the funeral director cannot withdraw those funds until the death of the arranger. However, the arranger can always withdraw the money and terminate the arrangements. Of course, any prearrangements you make may be useless if your heirs are unaware of them.

You, or your heirs, must determine whether or not you wish your body to be *embalmed.* Embalming is the process by which blood and body fluids are removed from the corpse and a preserving fluid injected into the arteries. An embalmed body is temporarily preserved from decay. Because a decaying body could cause disease, embalming is looked upon as a health measure. It also preserves the features of the body for viewing at an open-casket wake and/or funeral.

No state requires embalming if the burial or cremation occurs soon after death. However, if you intend to have an open casket wake or funeral, you must opt for embalming. On the other hand, if you do not intend to let people view your body after your death, whether or not to be embalmed is up to you. Tell your heirs your wishes.

You may have specific desires as to music, or no music, at your funeral; flowers, or no flowers; certain poetry, or no poetry; military, or nonmilitary procedures; or other specific rites. The forms in this chapter allow you to express these wishes.

## MEMORIAL SERVICES

*Memorial services,* as the term is used in this book, are similar to funeral services, except that the body of the deceased is not present. Instead, the body has already been buried, cremated, sent to a medical school, or perhaps even lost in a catastrophe. The deceased or the family may want to deal with the remains before holding formal services, or a memorial service may be held because family and friends are unable to gather immediately after death. Memorial services, like funeral services, can be religious or nonreligious in character. They can be held at a church, home, funeral home, rented hall, or any other place. They are in remembrance of, and with respect for, the deceased. If you prefer a memorial service rather than a funeral service, let your heirs know.

## FUNERAL AND MEMORIAL SOCIETIES

Funeral and memorial societies are nonprofit, volunteer-run organizations that have arisen throughout the country to provide members with simple, affordable funerals and disposition of remains. Many societies make prearrangements with local funeral homes for low-cost funerals, memorial services, burials, and cremations. Members, who pay a small membership fee (generally a one-time fee of $10–$25), can save hundreds of dollars on a cremation or thousands of dollars on a traditional funeral and burial. Societies usually advocate immediate cremation (without embalmment or funeral services) followed by a memorial service commemorating the deceased, and they provide their members with forms that they can use to express their preferences. At the time of death, members of the society assist the family in making arrangements. Depending on the laws of the particular state, a memorial society may be able to transfer the body from a hospital directly to a crematorium, or may only be able to give advice to the family.

For a list of funeral and memorial societies in the United States and Canada, send a self-addressed, stamped business-sized envelope with your request to Funeral and Memorial Societies of America, Inc. (P.O. Box 10, Hinesburg, VT 05461). There is no charge for the list, though a small contribution to cover costs is appreciated.

# My Final Wishes—General

I wish my body to:

☐ become an organ donor

☐ be bequeathed to a medical school.

☐ be buried in the earth.

☐ be entombed in a mausoleum.

☐ be cremated.

☐ any of the above as determined by my heirs.

I wish to have:

☐ a funeral service (body present).

☐ a memorial service (body not present).

☐ no service.

☐ any of the above.

I wish that a funeral, or memorial, service be held at:

☐ church.

☐ funeral home.

☐ my home.

☐ other: _____

_____

☐ any of the above.

My preferences are as follows (include address and phone #):

Name of house of worship: _____

_____

Religious leader's name: _____

_____

Funeral home: _____

_____

My obituary should appear in the following publications: _____

Location of obituary (optional): _____

☐ I am not a member of a memorial society.

☐ I am a member of a memorial society with which I have left my wishes as to the disposition of my remains. The name, address, and phone number is:

_____

_____

# Donation of Organs and Tissues

☐ I do not wish to donate any organs or tissues.

☐ I wish to donate any needed organs or tissues. *(If you are bequeathing your body to a medical school, only donate corneas from the eyes.)*

☐ I wish to donate only the following organs or tissues:

Organs | Tissues

☐ heart     ☐ blood vessels     ☐ heart valves

☐ kidneys     ☐ bone     ☐ inner ear

☐ liver     ☐ cartilage     ☐ intestines

☐ lungs     ☐ corneas from eyes     ☐ skin

☐ pancreas

☐ other: _____

_____

☐ Limitations or special wishes: _____

_____

_____

☐ I have executed a uniform donor card, and it is located: _____

_____

*Note:* The above donations will not be effective without the execution
of a uniform donor card and the approval of the next of kin.

❖❖❖❖❖❖

---

**UNIFORM DONOR CARD**

OF _____
*Print or type name of Donor*

In the hope that I may help others, I hereby make this anatomical gift, if medically acceptable, to take effect upon my death. The words and marks below indicate my desires.

I give: (a) _____ any needed organs or parts.
     (b) _____ only the following organs or parts:

_____
*Specify the organ(s) or part(s)*

for the purposes of transplantation, therapy, medical research, or education.

     (c) _____ my body for anatomical study if needed.

Limitations or special wishes if any: _____

_____

---

**UNIFORM DONOR CARD**

OF _____
*Print or type name of Donor*

In the hope that I may help others, I hereby make this anatomical gift, if medically acceptable, to take effect upon my death. The words and marks below indicate my desires.

I give: (a) _____ any needed organs or parts.
     (b) _____ only the following organs or parts:

_____
*Specify the organ(s) or part(s)*

for the purposes of transplantation, therapy, medical research, or education.

     (c) _____ my body for anatomical study if needed.

Limitations or special wishes if any: _____

_____

---

*The uniform donor cards above may be removed from the book to be carried in a wallet or purse.*
*Both sides of a card must be completed, signed, and witnessed to be valid.*

# Bequeathal to a Medical School

☐ I wish my body to be bequeathed to:

Medical school: _____

Address and phone #: _____

_____

*and/or*

☐ any other medical school if inconvenient to send to the above, or, if not needed by the above.

I ☐ have or ☐ have not made prearrangements with the above medical school.

I realize that sometimes the above arrangements cannot be carried out. My alternative desire is for:

    ☐ burial or entombment

    ☐ cremation

and I have filled out the pertinent portion of these forms in case an alternative to body bequeathal is necessary.

☐ I have executed a uniform donor card, and it is located: _____

_____

*Note:* The above body bequest will not be effective without the execution of a uniform donor card and the approval of the next of kin.

❖ ❖ ❖ ❖ ❖ ❖

| Signed by the donor and the following two witnesses in the presence of each other. | | Signed by the donor and the following two witnesses in the presence of each other. | |
|---|---|---|---|
| _____ | _____ | _____ | _____ |
| *Signature of Donor* | *Date of Birth* | *Signature of Donor* | *Date of Birth* |
| _____ | _____ | _____ | _____ |
| *City & State* | *Date Signed* | *City & State* | *Date Signed* |
| _____ | _____ | _____ | _____ |
| *Witness* | *Witness* | *Witness* | *Witness* |
| This is a legal document under the Uniform Anatomical Gift Act or similar laws. | | This is a legal document under the Uniform Anatomical Gift Act or similar laws. | |

*The uniform donor cards above may be removed from the book to be carried in a wallet or purse. Both sides of a card must be completed, signed, and witnessed to be valid.*

# Burial or Entombment

☐ I do not own, nor have legal use of, a cemetery lot or mausoleum crypt.

☐ I ☐ own  or ☐ have legal use of:

   ☐ a cemetery lot

   ☐ a mausoleum crypt

The ownership of the lot or crypt is in the name of: _____

_____

The lot or crypt is located at:

   Cemetery or mausoleum: _____

   Address and phone #: _____

   Section: _____Lot #: _____

   Other description: _____

   _____

   Location of deed: _____

I desire a ☐ grave marker  or ☐ monument.

In addition to my name, date of birth, and date of death, I would like the following to be placed

thereon: _____

_____

_____

Special instructions:

_____

_____

_____

_____

_____

_____

_____

# Cremation

☐ I wish my body to be cremated immediately.

☐ I wish my body to be cremated immediately and a memorial service subsequently held.

☐ I wish my body to be cremated following a funeral service.

☐ I wish my body to be cremated, but I leave the other details to my heirs.

Following my cremation, I wish my ashes:

☐ to be scattered (where permitted by law): _____

_____

☐ to be placed in an urn and buried, or entombed: _____

_____

☐ to be handled as my heirs determine

# Funeral or Memorial Service

*(You can continue any of the below on the next page.)*

I wish the service to be for: ☐ friends and relatives ☐ private or ☐ other:_____

_____

I prefer that a wake be held for ☐ one day ☐ two days ☐ not at all ☐ other: _____

I wish the casket to be: ☐ open ☐ closed    I prefer to wear: _____

My favorite hymns/music are: _____

_____

Soloist: _____

My favorite scriptures, poems, etc., are: _____

_____

I ☐ do or ☐ do not wish flowers.

Disposal of flowers: _____

☐ I am a member of the following organization (military veterans, Masons, etc.) and desire an organization service (specify name of organization): _____

I request that memorial contributions be made to: _____

I ☐ do or ☐ do not wish to be embalmed.

I ☐ do or ☐ do not wish to have an interment service at graveside.

I wish my funeral expenses to be: ☐ minimal ☐ low average ☐ average

☐ high average or ☐ not limited

I prefer the following funeral home (include address and phone #): _____

_____

I ☐ have or ☐ have not made funeral prearrangements with the funeral home.

I ☐ have or ☐ have not made any prepayment of funeral expenses.

If I have made any prepayment, it is a follows: _____

_____

_____

_____

# Funeral or Memorial Service *(continued)*

_____

_____

_____

_____

_____

_____

_____

_____

_____

_____

_____

_____

_____

_____

_____

_____

_____

_____

_____

_____

_____

_____

_____

# CHAPTER 11

# *Explaining Additional Information*

When you have completed all of the preceding forms, you might wish to list other information for your heirs. Only you know what that may be. For example, perhaps you wish that certain papers or letters be destroyed without being opened. If so, tell your heirs about it. Maybe you have personal messages that you wish relayed to people after your death. The forms in this chapter provide a place to do that. In other words, use them as you see fit.

❖❖❖❖❖❖

*Keep this book up-to-date.*

*Share it with your heirs.*

❖❖❖❖❖❖

*GOOD LUCK AND GOOD HEALTH!*

# Notes for My Heirs

_____

_____

_____

_____

_____

_____

_____

_____

_____

_____

_____

_____

_____

_____

_____

_____

_____

_____

_____

❖❖❖❖❖❖

Please destroy the following items without opening or reading them: _____

_____

_____

❖❖❖❖❖❖

# Notes for My Heirs *(continued)*

# Notes for My Heirs *(continued)*

# Notes for My Heirs *(continued)*

# Notes for My Heirs *(continued)*

---

---

---

---

---

---

---

---

---

---

---

---

---

---

---

---

---

---

---

---

---

---

---

---

---

---

---

---

---

# Notes for My Heirs *(continued)*

# Notes for My Heirs *(continued)*

_____

_____

_____

_____

_____

_____

_____

_____

_____

_____

_____

_____

_____

_____

_____

_____

_____

_____

_____

_____

_____

_____

_____

_____

_____

_____

# Index